VOTER Z

JENNIFER LAMBERT

NEW DEGREE PRESS

VOTER Z

ISBN   978-1-63676-917-2 *Paperback*
        978-1-63676-981-3 *Kindle Ebook*
        978-1-63730-085-5 *Ebook*

To my dad, Jim, who taught me to never give up on my dreams.

To my mom, Janet, who embodies courage.

To my sister, Rachel, who never fails to make me smile.

CONTENTS

"*The earth belongs always to the living generation. They may manage it then, and what proceeds from it, as they please, during their usufruct.*"

—THOMAS JEFFERSON

PART 1

INTRODUCTION TO GEN Z

1

WINTER

As the eldest cohort of Generation Z entered their teenage years, many residents of the United States strived to figure out what events and beliefs defined these young Americans. For the purposes of this book, Generation Z (also known as "Gen Z") is defined as Americans born between the years 1995 and 2012. I chose 1995 as the start date for this generation, as many other generational researchers have done before me, due to the idea that people born in 1995 were only in kindergarten in September of 2001. They had not yet developed a level of societal consciousness that would allow them to understand the magnitude of an event like 9/11. Many scholars debate over what the end date is for Generation Z. I chose 2012 because it is the year in which the Sandy Hook shooting occurred and Trayvon Martin was murdered. These events were turning points in American political discourse, igniting a gun control movement centered around American schoolchildren and a social and political movement declaring that yes, Black lives matter.

Gen Zers are often characterized in national discourse by their constant exposure to technology, high stress levels, and the "coddled" nature of their upbringing. The "coddled" assumption derives from the negative label some have adopted for Gen Z: "the participation trophy generation." This label attempts to mock Gen Zers for growing up in a society that equally rewards effort and victory. It fails to account for the hardships many Gen Zers, particularly those who are people of color, have faced growing up in America in the 21st century. An example is the financial challenges of coming of age during a time when income inequality was rapidly increasing across the country.[1]

The pervading characterizations of Gen Z miss the point of what has uniquely positioned this generation to enact sweeping changes in their workplaces, in schools, and in bastions of political power. These young people have lived through terrorist attacks on their home soil, the 2008 and 2020 recessions, the two impeachment trials of Donald Trump, countless mass shootings, and a pandemic all before many of them reached their mid-20s. These young Americans also organized a march on Washington, built followings of millions on social media, and are now setting record highs for youth voter turnout.[2] They reject the status quo of the world they were born into, but with every passing day they have succeeded in creating movements to change it. Generation

---

1   Elise Gould, "Decades of Rising Economic Inequality in the U.S.," *Economic Policy Institute,* March 27, 2019.

2   Emily Witt, "How the Survivors of Parkland Began the Never Again Movement," *The New Yorker,* February 19, 2018. Taylor Lorenz, "Hype House and the Los Angeles TikTok Mansion Gold Rush," *The New York Times,* January 3, 2020. Kelly Beadle et al., "Election Week 2020: Young People Increase Turnout, Lead Biden to Victory," *Tuft University Center for Information and Research on Civic Learning and Engagement,* November 25, 2020.

Zers have a unique mindset for growth that originates from their status as the most educated and diverse generation in American history.[3] The eldest members of Generation Z have the capacity to be a political force that changes the American political system.

This book will focus on the eldest cohort of Generation Z living in the United States, those born between 1995 and 2004, who were at least entering their mid-teenage years during the 2020 election cycle. Those Gen Zers who are born between 2005 and 2012 are likely to exhibit similar behaviors to their elder generational counterparts; however, at the time this book was written, those born in 2005 were just entering their mid-teenage years. This is a time when their long-term political beliefs are just beginning to take shape. Therefore, it is essential to focus on the eldest Gen Zers, who are deeply invested in the process of affirming their belief systems. In my research, I found this age group has a collective memory of certain core events that have informed their worldview and acted as agents of their political socialization.

These events span the time period from their earliest political memories in the years 2006–2008 to 2021. The exposure of the eldest Gen Zers to key historical events at the peak of their impressionability have turned them into engaged citizens who fight for a more just, inclusive American society.

These events include:
- The Iraq War

---

3   Kim Parker and Ruth Igielnik, "On the Cusp of Adulthood and Facing an Uncertain Future: What We Know about Gen Z So Far," *Pew Research Center,* May 14, 2020.

- The Great Recession
- The Sandy Hook shooting
- The Parkland shooting
- The Supreme Court's decision in *Obergefell v. Hodges* (2015)
- The Black Lives Matter movement
- The election and two impeachments of Donald Trump
- The coronavirus pandemic and resulting recession
- The reason these events bear such significance to Rebuilders, the elder cohort of Gen Zers, has to do with their timing, wide circulation of news coverage surrounding them, and the passionate discourse prompted by them.

GENERATIONAL THEORY

According to generational theorists Neil Howe and William Strauss, Americans born between 1995 and 2004 are part of a "hero" generation that will team up to survive a crisis period in the United States.[4] The Strauss-Howe Generational Theory, also called the "Fourth Turning" claims American history occurs in eighty-year cycles.[5] Each cycle is composed of four twenty yearlong turnings, with each turning being equivalent to a weather season.[6]

---

4   William Strauss and Neil Howe, *The Fourth Turning: An American Prophecy – What the Cycles of History Tell Us about America's Next Rendezvous with Destiny* (New York: Crown, 2009).

5   Ibid.

6   Ibid

CURRENT CYCLE

FIRST TURNING (ALSO CALLED THE "SPRING" OR "HIGH")
- During highs, institutions are strong, and individualism is weak[7]
- Spanned the post-World War II era and happy days of the 1950s[8]
- Ended with the assassination of JFK, which served as a violent end to the idealism that reigned during that American high[9]

SECOND TURNING (THE "SUMMER" OR "AWAKENING")[10]
- During awakenings, institutions come under heavy scrutiny due to a renewed push for personal autonomy[11]
- The second turning ended with the tax revolts of the early 1980s that propelled Ronald Reagan to political superstardom[12]

THIRD TURNING (THE "FALL" OR "UNRAVELING")[13]
- During unravelings, the institutions attacked during awakenings become weak as individualism thrives and distrust of government grows[14]
- Came about quietly through the culture wars of the 1980s and the long economic boom of the 1990s[15]

---

7   Ibid.
8   Ibid.
9   Ibid.
10 Ibid.
11 Ibid.
12 Ibid.
13 Ibid.
14 Ibid.
15 Ibid.

- The third turning came to a startling halt in 2008 with the onset of the Great Recession[16]

FOURTH TURNING (THE "WINTER" OR "CRISIS")[17]

- Americans are currently living through the fourth turning[18]
- During crises, the institutions that had been weakened are scrapped and revamped as America deals with some kind of calamity that could threaten the nation's survival[19]
- America will remain in this crisis period until 2030[20]
- The eldest members of Generation Z are uniquely positioned to play a key role in surviving this crisis period

DEFINING GENERATION Z

Despite having experienced different world events during their impressionable years, the eldest half of Generation Z does share some of the same "hero" traits as the Millennial generation. Both cohorts are teaming up with their peers to survive the current crisis period and revive the civic backbone of America. As Neil Howe said, there are "symbiotic relationships between historical events and how these generations react, shape, or cause these events as a direct consequence of these generational archetypes."[21] Strauss and Howe's classify babies born in 1995–2004 as part of the Millennial generation,

16 Ibid.
17 Ibid.
18 Ibid.
19 Ibid.
20 Ibid.
21 *Hedgeye*, "The Fourth Turning: Why American 'Crisis' May Last until 2030," April 1, 2017, YouTube Video, 14:42.

but some distinct characteristics separate the eldest Gen Zers from Millennials.[22]

I believe lumping late 1990s and early 2000s babies with Americans born in the 1980s misrepresents the events that have forged each cohort. The events that occur when one is coming of age matter greatly in terms of the shared generational outlook they create. These events, the discourse surrounding them, and our reactions to them help shape an individual's political belief system when they enter their teenage years.

For example, people born in 1995–2004 cannot remember what life is like without the internet or before 9/11. Their digital nativism makes them advanced technological communicators who value swiftness and transparency. The experience of growing up in a post-9/11 world has exposed them to the realities of war, terrorism, and foreign policy through the lens of conflicts based in the Middle East. This worldview formed the foundation of their political belief systems. This collective generational outlook based around certain historical events of the 2000s and 2010s distinguishes Gen Z from the true Millennials of the 1980s and early 1990s. Millennials had already begun, and in some cases completed, the work of forming the basis for their respective political belief systems based on world events prior to 9/11. While political belief systems can change over the course of a lifetime, Americans are most likely to adopt long-lasting political beliefs between the ages of sixteen and twenty-two.[23] During this time period,

---

22 Ibid.

23 "Political Socialization," University of Minnesota Libraries, accessed January 5, 2020.

"younger people have less clearly defined political beliefs, which makes them more likely to be influenced by key societal events."[24]

CONCEPTS AND METHODOLOGY

The term "Americans" will be used in this book exclusively to refer to residents of the United States of America. The label of "progressive" will be used in this book to refer to political ideologies that focus on social progress and thus will not be used solely as a synonym for the political left. The terms "GOP" and "the right" will be used to refer to the Republican Party. "The left" will be used to refer to the Democratic Party. References to areas as "red" indicate a general Republican lean in that area's electorate. References to areas as "blue" indicate a general Democratic lean in that area's electorate. While I will be using the term "Gen Z" throughout this book, any findings or generalizations presented about this group are based off of my research on the 1995 to 2004 cohort. Younger Gen Zers have not yet reached the age where they are most politically impressionable so it is not yet possible to determine what their political belief systems look like; however, there is reason to believe they will share many traits with their older generational peers.

This book will tell the story of the subset of Generation Zers born from 1995 to 2004, who I have dubbed the "Rebuilding Generation," to figure out how the young heroes of this crisis period formed the belief systems that remain at the heart of their quest to reconstruct weakened American

---

24   Ibid.

institutions. The reason I chose the name the "Rebuilding Generation" is because these elder Gen Zers will be tasked with the work of reviving the civic backbone of American society in the post-crisis period. They will have to retain the lessons key historical events of the 2000s, 2010s, and early 2020s taught them so they can reshape their communities and systems of government to better address systemic issues. They are well-educated, skeptical of the current government, and putting in the work heroes are expected to do during a crisis period. They overwhelmingly disapprove of Donald Trump, want a bigger, more efficient federal government, and care about the lasting effects of gun control, climate change, income inequality, and racial injustice in America.

I spoke to members of what I call the Rebuilding Generation's activist class, the ones most likely to pursue a career in politics and run for office, for this book. I solicited survey responses from about forty of these Rebuilders and conducted in-depth interviews with twenty of them. These subjects were found via a variety of methods. Many of them came from Twitter, where I examined youth political discourse to find those users most likely to facilitate conversation and debate, and some came from my own personal connections to political science students. These interviews were not random. I carefully selected them to represent a diverse range of home states, sexual orientations, gender identities, religions, races, ethnic backgrounds, and political views. These interviews, along with my own personal experiences growing up as a Generation Zer and my political science education, inform the content in this book.

ABOUT THIS BOOK

This book is the result of my effort to understand the collective political identity of this generation and the major events, beliefs, and cultural phenomena that have shaped America's young citizens into a strong political force. This book seeks to delve into the formative events that shaped this generation's political beliefs in an attempt to understand how this generation will go about rehabilitating America's economic, governmental, and social institutions. Those memories include the Sandy Hook and Parkland shootings, the elections of Barack Obama and Donald Trump, the death of Trayvon Martin, the Supreme Court's decision in *Obergefell v. Hodges* (2015), the fallout from the Iraq War, and the COVID-19 pandemic. These events and the national discourse that surrounded them shaped Rebuilders' outlook on America's political system.

The primary political socialization of this generational cohort occurred around the 2016 Presidential election, giving them a bleak outlook on the American political system as a whole. The first political campaigns they truly followed occurred in 2016, when two candidates with dismal favorability ratings ran for office and were simultaneously ensnared in personal, political, and legal controversies.

The presidency of Donald Trump has thrown this mostly progressive generation for a loop, forcing them to reconcile their perception of the world with the reality of America's dysfunctional political, financial, and social institutions.[25]

---

25   Claire Hansen, "Young Voters Turned Out in Historic Numbers, Early Estimates Show," *U.S. News*, November 7, 2018.

This is not to say all Gen Zers are anti-Trump; 26 percent of young Americans surveyed by Harvard's Institute of Politics for their Election 2020 Youth Poll supported Trump in the presidential contest.[26] That is still an overwhelming amount of youth support for Joe Biden, especially considering his status as a challenger to an incumbent president. In later chapters, the different political views of Gen Zers will be examined to show how young voters are pushing for both major political parties to adopt more progressive policy ideas.

My goal with this book is to fill the gap between generational theory and American political reality. My desire is to illustrate how exactly the Rebuilding Generation (as a cohort of Generation Z) has, and will continue to, live up to the "hero" archetype that Howe and Strauss forecasted over two decades ago. As a political science student, I find most of my academic coursework focuses on the study of past and present institutional leadership without focusing on the trajectory of these institutions and their leaders. It's the nature of academic political scientists to resist conducting research with the aim of predicting future outcomes, although they do explore trends and theories that hint at potential shifts in political and economic institutions.

WHAT COMES NEXT?

It is essential to American political discourse that the identities and beliefs of youth activists, voters, and future leaders are understood—especially as Generation Z bursts onto the

---

26 "Harvard Youth Poll: Election 2020," Harvard Kennedy School Institute of Politics, Published October 26, 2020. https://iop.harvard.edu/youth-poll/harvard-youth-poll.

national stage as they lead protests, spearhead mass mobilization efforts, and take to the voting booth. As a member of Generation Z, I believe I can authentically tell the story of my generational peers who I have been studying since the day I was born. I know this story because I am part of it. I have spent the past twenty years of my life living and breathing the experiences of Generation Z. I feel it is my responsibility to encapsulate the spirit of my generation and to tell the stories of my peers to fill a gap in knowledge that can only be filled by a Gen Z voice.

Profiles of current activists among Generation Z, like the Parkland students who organized the March for Our Lives and Malala, who launched an international movement for women's rights and education, demonstrate the radical change this generation's members are capable of enacting when their voices are heard. Deep dives into the politicians who inspire this generation like fellow "heroes" in Millennials, such as Alexandria Ocasio-Cortez and Pete Buttigieg, and Gen Zers like Madison Cawthorn, show that this generation values authenticity, frankness, and energy in its leaders.

The activists of the Rebuilding Generation compose the next class of American leaders who will usher in a new "high" as the next cycle of American history begins around the year 2030.[27] To understand how that next "high" will turn out, Americans have to take a long look at the key events in the unraveling and crisis periods that have shaped Generation Z's collective outlook. It is also important to examine the ways

---

27 *Hedgeye,* "The Fourth Turning: Why American 'Crisis' May Last until 2030," April 1, 2017, YouTube Video, 14:42.

those beliefs have manifested themselves in the middle of the crisis. This will paint a picture of the sweeping changes the Rebuilding Generation hopes to enact at the tail-end of this crisis period or "winter."

First, Americans will have to endure through the current crisis that has resulted from the coronavirus pandemic and the corresponding recession. Then, the Rebuilding Generation will live up to its name by cleaning up the aftermath. It is a terrifying and overwhelming burden for young Americans to shoulder. Neil Howe argues fourth turnings are essential to a functioning society: "And just as forests need fires and rivers need floods, so does society need events which clean out the debris…something which tilts the whole playing field of power and wealth from the old back to the young. This is what Fourth Turnings do; they renew us. Fourth Turnings are the price we must pay for a new golden age."[28]

America is in the dead of winter, the actual "crisis" of the crisis period/fourth turning. The next and final step of the fourth turning is the resolution. It is the hope on the horizon that Americans will successfully rebuild the country's institutions in a way that revitalizes civic life and sets a post-crisis order that will withstand the next four to six decades. The Rebuilding Generation will be at the forefront of determining what that post-crisis order will look like.

This book will shed light on the formation and implementation of those values among the future leaders in the

---

28 Ibid.

Rebuilding Generation who will guide America into the next cycle of its historical life.

2

ZBELLION

Who are the next generation of leaders that will rebuild America after this crisis period ends? Generation Z is remarkably adept at messaging and organizing. They have been cultivating their own personal brands since the minute they signed up for their first social media account. Personal branding skills, which this generation has in spades, are highly transferrable to political organizing. A penchant for mass mobilization combined with record high levels of civic engagement gives Gen Z the capacity to upend the political system as it currently exists. The attitudes and beliefs undergirding this generation are propelling them to challenge the existing political establishment and one day, become leaders in their own right. Therefore, it is crucial Americans comprehend the origins of their vision for a more just, equitable America. It's time to stop discounting these young people and understand what events and beliefs have shaped the ideologies of future American leaders.

This chapter will delve into why Generation Z has a deep distrust of governmental and financial institutions. This sentiment prompted the Pentagon to create a hypothetical war scenario in which Gen Zers launched a domestic rebellion in the year 2025; they call it "Zbellion."[29] Through the lens of the Great Recession and the coronavirus pandemic, this chapter will explore how Gen Z was first exposed to systemic inequalities in the United States and why these experiences have made them committed to the work of remedying them. While Generation Z is unlikely to launch an actual domestic rebellion, they are beginning to use their increasing political clout to shape the public agenda.

In their own way, Gen Zers are launching a rebellion against the status quo for reasons not dissimilar to what the Pentagon laid out in their war game. The scenario crafted by the Pentagon includes background on the "Zbellion" that is not far from the conclusions this book will draw about the origins of Gen Z's rampant discontent with the current American political system:

> Both the September 11 terrorist attacks and the Great Recession greatly influenced the attitudes of this generation in the United States, and resulted in a feeling of unsettlement and insecurity among Gen Z. Although Millennials experienced these events during their coming of age, Gen Z lived through them as part of their childhood, affecting their realism and world view ...many found themselves stuck with excessive college debt

---

29 Nick Turse, "Pentagon War Game Includes Scenario for Military Response to Domestic Gen Z Rebellion," *The Intercept*, June 5, 2020.

when they discovered employment options did not meet their expectations. Gen Z are often described as seeking independence and opportunity but are also among the least likely to believe there is such a thing as the 'American Dream,' and that the 'system is rigged' against them. Frequently seeing themselves as agents for social change, they crave fulfillment and excitement in their job to help 'move the world forward.'[30]

—NICK TURSE

This worldview, shaped by a general lack of faith in the government and financial institutions to act in the public interest, is unique to Generation Z and has resulted in their desire to be changemakers. Gen Z are (unfairly) thought of as practically identical to Millennials. The key difference lies in the fact many Millennials had a chance at achieving the American Dream before the Great Recession stripped them of key opportunities to accrue wealth.[31] Millennials had hopes of paying off their student loans, earning an appropriate salary, and one day buying a house of their own; however, increasing unemployment and a downturn in the economy at the start of their careers means "their salaries are 20 percent less, in real terms, than what their Baby Boomer parents were making at the same age."[32]

30 Ibid.
31 Corey Seemiller and Meghan Grace, *Generation Z: A Century in the Making*, (New York: Routledge, 2019), 10.
32 Ibid.

Rebuilders are likely to face a similar fate. The oldest members of Gen Z were about eleven when the financial crisis began, and it has had a profound effect on their financial habits as well as their views on the role the economy plays in both domestic and global politics. Before Gen Zers could even dream of an ideal future, they watched as their parents and other relatives were laid off, struggled to pay bills, and lost years of savings. Even in the aftermath of the Great Recession, the increasing income inequality, student debt, and cost of living in the United States pose threats to the future financial security of Gen Z.

I recall conversations about classic works like *The Death of a Salesman*, *Of Mice and Men*, and *A Raisin in the Sun* leading to incredibly depressing yet refreshingly honest conversations about our generation's inability to realize the American Dream. The dream for Gen Zers is earning a degree from an accredited institution without accruing a crushing amount of student loan debt and going on to make enough money on a starting salary to afford an apartment with an actual bedroom. Sadly, this is especially challenging for Gen Zers who are people of color (POC) due to the fact they earn less than their white counterparts.[33]

***

The reason the Great Recession is such an important agent of political socialization, to the extent the Pentagon names it as a potential catalyst for the revolutionary attitudes of an

33   Robert Manduca, "Income Inequality and the Persistence of Racial Economic Disparities," *Sociological Science* 5, no. 3 (March 2018): 183.

entire generation, is because it exposed systemic injustices and the instability of the financial market. For Gen Zers, economic inequality is a racial justice issue. These Gen Zers believe archaic institutions and out-of-touch leaders have done very little to address systemic inequalities (particularly along racial and socioeconomic lines) in the United States.

The Great Recession of 2008 and the bailout of major financial institutions and corporations sowed seeds of distrust even in the minds of the youngest Americans. Gen Zers were just beginning to come into political consciousness in 2008. It was not just middle- and lower-class Americans who were hit by the effects of a rapidly declining economy. Rich Americans also took a few years to recover from the Great Recession, showing that income inequality had not yet made them immune to the financial impacts of a global economic collapse. The American public hardly had time to catch their breath from the last financial collapse before the next storm rolled in: the recession resulting from the coronavirus pandemic.

The coronavirus recession, which began in 2020, has reinforced the feelings of "unsettlement and insecurity" outlined in the Zbellion scenario.[34] While the economy began to rebound in the mid-2010s and sustained stable growth for several years, no one could have predicted it could once again come to a grinding halt.[35] The pandemic has been an unexpected global catastrophe that has once again plunged America into a state of economic disrepair. Mass unemployment

---

34   Turse, "Pentagon War Game."

35   Josh Barro, "3 Big Economic Trends of the 2010s," *New York Magazine*, December 30, 2019.

and dramatic changes in business models have completely disrupted the workforce. The pandemic has exposed disparities in access to quality, affordable healthcare.

The economic recovery so far has shown that billionaires are quick to rebound from pandemic-induced downturns in the market while working class Americans face layoffs and the prospect of eviction in the absence of concrete financial assistance from the federal government. Billionaires are getting richer while the middle and lower classes get poorer. According to Chuck Collins, who studies economic inequality at the Institute for Policy Studies, "On March 18, 2020, the total wealth of US billionaires was $2.947 trillion. As of November 17, 2020, total U.S. billionaire wealth has increased $960 billion to $3.907 trillion."[36]

The number of US billionaires has increased from 614 in March to 647 today, an increase of thirty-three people.[37] A later chapter in this book will delve into the crushing blow dealt to middle- and lower-class Americans by the pandemic, but for now it is sufficient to say many of them struggled to survive while billionaires and millionaires thrived. For years to come, the failure of the government to provide adequate support to ailing Americans as they lost their jobs, homes, and lives will be remembered by Generation Z. It is no wonder Generation Zers are distrustful of governmental and financial institutions as they witnessed inaction while

---

36 Bianca Agustin, Chuck Collins, Jonathan Heller, Sara Myklebust, and Omar Ocampo, *Billionaire Wealth vs. Community Health: Protecting Essential Workers*, (Washington, D.C.: Institute for Policy Studies, 2020).

37 Ibid.

so many of them and their families stood on the edge of economic and medical collapse.

Students who graduated college in the early 2020s, an overwhelming majority of whom are Gen Zers, find themselves entering a job market that is similarly bleak to that of 2008. Current college students struggle to make the most of a virtual education while dealing with on-campus outbreaks, semesters with no breaks, strict isolation rules, and canceled internships. It is hard to forecast the exact implications of this recession, but it is certain it will impact the economic prospects of Gen Z by affecting their professional development opportunities and entry-level job prospects.

***

Gen Zers are utilizing their increasing political clout to demand government officials act in key policy areas. Political campaigns are beginning to cater more and more to Gen Z and Millennials as they come to comprise the largest part of the American electorate. Millennials and Gen Zers, the most progressive generations within the American electorate, are forcing politicians to move left and could cause the first political realignment in America since Reagan's first presidential election. It is important to note I use the term "progressive" not to mean a strictly left-leaning view, but to indicate a move toward social progress on both sides of the aisle.

Republican and Democrat Gen Zers alike believe the government should take a more active role in addressing societal issues, indicating a bipartisan push for the expanded role of government.[38] These progressive beliefs include wide-sweeping reforms and regulations principally aimed at creating a more equitable society where the American dream is revived. This means calling for equal access to higher education opportunities, increases in the minimum wage, immediate action to prevent climate change, gun control measures, and fair taxation of all economic classes. It also includes positive, constructive reform of governmental, financial, and industrial institutions in order to create a more just American society.

This moment in history, the beginning of the post-Trump era, is a flashpoint and Gen Zers are not going to take it lightly because it will determine the course of their future. These young Americans are transforming the political discourse in the United States by forcing conversations on controversial issues which will force both major parties to re-examine their policy platforms. Gen Zers are a political force of nature and refuse to be ignored any longer. While it is impossible to predict the nature of a post-crisis America, I do not think Gen Z's political power should be underestimated. Young Americans have been notoriously involved with some of the most successful social movements in American history including the LGBTQ+ movement, Civil Rights Movement, and now they could be mobilizing their peers to vote in the largest numbers ever recorded. When America enters the next phase of its history at the close of the 2020s, it will be Gen Zers assuming positions of power.

38   Kim Parker and Ruth Igielnik, "On the Cusp of Adulthood and Facing an Uncertain Future: What We Know about Gen Z So Far," *Pew Research Center*, May 14, 2020.

PART II

KNOWING ME,
KNOWING Z

3

THE HOMELAND GENERATION

What defines Generation Z? As researchers launched efforts to study the babies born just before and after the start of the new millennium, they searched for an appropriate moniker for this new generation. Generation Z did not yet have a nickname like "Millennials," "Baby Boomers," or the "Silent Generation." Suggestions for Gen Z's nickname included iGen, Post-Millennials, Digital Natives, Founders, Zoomers, the Hopeful Generation, the Anxious Generation, the Meme Generation, and the Delta Generation.[39] So far, none of these names have been popular enough to act as a permanent label. Generation Z has been stuck with its generic alphabetical tag, not unlike "Generation X." One nickname that did stick out among the rest, and that many researchers have employed when making references to Generation Z, is "Homelanders,"

---

39 Corey Seemiller and Meghan Grace, *Generation Z: A Century in the Making*, (New York: Routledge, 2019), xx.

a name first adopted by generational theorists William Strauss and Neil Howe.

Neil Howe described the process of choosing a generational label: "We conducted an online contest in 2006 to name the generation coming after the Millennials. Several different names were suggested and voted on. Homeland Generation became the ultimate winner."[40] Howe further explained the label of "Homelanders" arose from the fact Generation Z came of age after the creation of the Homeland Security Department and during the War on Terror.[41] These events played a major role in shaping Gen Zers' collective generational outlook. This chapter will explore the roles 9/11 and the War on Terror played in the political socialization of Generation Z's elder cohort, the Rebuilders, and how it has led them to favor anti-interventionist foreign policy.

It is important to point out the people I interviewed for this novel spanned the age range of 1995 to 2004, placing them in the peculiar situation of exhibiting the characteristics of the Homeland generation while not being placed in Howe's exact generational timeframe. Howe's generational timeframe places the beginning of the Homeland generation around 2000 to 2006.[42] This differs slightly from my timeframe which places the beginning of this generation around the year 1995. Those born between 1995 and 2000 can be thought of as generational cuspers, or Zillennials, straddling the Millennial and Homeland Generations.

---

40   Neil Howe, "Introducing the Homeland Generation," *Forbes*, October 27, 2014.

41   Ibid.

42   Ibid.

Strauss and Howe were also responsible for coining the name "Millennials" for Generation Y. I believe it is important to include those born from 1995 to 2000 in the discussion of the Homeland Generation because these Americans do not have memories of political events before 9/11 happened. Therefore, their worldview has also been shaped by the post-9/11 political landscape.

Rebuilders have memories of growing up in America under strict homeland protection policies and ever-expanding surveillance programs but have grown to be disillusioned by foreign policy of the War on Terror era. This has led the eldest members of Gen Z, the Rebuilders, to be overwhelmingly in favor of diplomatic actions instead of military intervention.[43] While Howe has argued that fallout from 9/11, the Iraq and Afghan War, and the rise of ISIS have formed the background to Generation Z's lives, these events were not equally significant in the political socialization of all Generation Zers. These events play more significant roles in the political identities of Generation Zers who have personal connections to those who died, were injured, or acted as first responders during the 9/11 attacks or fought in the subsequent wars.

This is a result of personal connections escalating these Iraq and Afghan wars and 9/11 from agents of political socialization to core memories. They no longer merely act as a historical backdrop. The discourse surrounding these events also becomes intensely personal and emotional as it intersects with anecdotes to form an oral history of the events. This

---

43 Pew Research Center, "The Generation Gap in American Politics," *Pew Research Center*, March 1, 2018.

kind of personal tie to a historical event enlarges its role in the political socialization process. This does not mean Gen Zers who lack personal connections to 9/11 or the wars in the Middle East have not been affected by them, but simply that they do not develop beliefs built on personal memories and emotions attached to these events.

Rebuilders have had their beliefs about foreign policy issues, including military intervention and the role of diplomacy, shaped by the War on Terror. These experiences include living with the constant fear of further escalations of conflicts with enemy nation states, feeling unsafe on American soil, or the consuming media reports about the Iraq and Afghan conflicts and the United States' continued presence in the Middle East. It is through the lens of these Middle East conflicts that Gen Zers came to understand the role of the United States in the international arena.

***

Gen Zers lack first-hand memories of 9/11, but their opinions on global actors have been shaped by its aftermath. The majority of Generation Z was born after the fateful September morning that changed the United States and the world forever. The eldest Gen Zers were all less than six years old when the twin towers came down. They have no recollection of them standing tall amongst the other skyscrapers that compose the New York City skyline. When the first plane struck the North Tower, my dad was feeding me mashed carrots while I sat in a highchair. Gen Zers only know moments of silence, memorials, and secondhand accounts of the day told from the perspective of their relatives. It is through these oral histories that many Gen Zers have constructed their understandings of that disastrous September day.

The majority of Gen Zers have never walked through the airport to catch a plane without being asked to take off their shoes, put their personal belongings through an x-ray machine, walk through a metal detector, and often face a dehumanizing and invasive pat-down afterwards. The threat of terrorist attacks in the United States has been omnipresent in their lives, and they have accepted it as a terrifying reality. On a plane, in a subway, at a concert, at a marathon, at church, at temple, at a nightclub, there is always a creeping fear something terrible could happen. This feeling is not unique to Gen Zers, but it is exacerbated for them because they have witnessed these terrorist attacks at young ages when they are the most impressionable. This creates a situation wherein "adolescents and young adults may have a more lasting effect on their worldview as many lack the experience and perspective to realize that the world isn't always in a state of conflict."[44] All Gen Zers know is a post-9/11 world.

They continue to mourn the America they never got to know before it. Rebuilders came of age during wartime, they watched as ISIS grew its presence in the Middle East, and they celebrated when Osama Bin Laden was killed (even if they did not fully understand his role in the War on Terror at the time). The very youngest subset of Gen Zers were not yet born when Seal Team Six raided Bin Laden's compound in Abbottabad, Pakistan. As a generation, they have been desensitized to violent attacks and disillusioned by the wars

---

44 Seemiller and Grace, *Generation Z: A Century in the Making*, 18.

that sought to put a stop to them. Existing global tensions have persisted over almost the entire course of Rebuilders' lifetime thus far. Conflicts between global powers are less about minuscule flare-ups or slight escalations, but rather an ongoing series of provocations that lead to sustained periods of unrest. This has shaped the generational outlook of Rebuilders to view the world as a place "where ongoing global tensions are simply the way of life."[45]

Despite these emotional attachments to the tragedy of 9/11, Jacob Pride voiced his belief that Generation Z is "closer to indifferent [about the War on Terror] than older generations who were maybe at least in high school during Operation Shock and Awe." He also mentioned how he feels about 9/11 fading out of the collective American consciousness, as the year 2021 marks the twentieth anniversary of that tragic day. Events that tend to evoke more emotion from Gen Z are the Boston Marathon bombing or the Sandy Hook shooting. Ask any member of Gen Z where they were when either of those events happened and they have a story ready to tell you.

While older generations like the Baby Boomers are more supportive of military intervention overseas, Gen Zers and Millennials are less likely to support foreign interventions. In a poll by Pew Research Center, 77 percent of Millennials agree with the idea that "good diplomacy is the best way to ensure peace."[46] This is in contrast to the 59 percent of Gen Xers, 52 percent of Baby Boomers, and 43 percent of Silents

---

45   Ibid.
46   Pew Research Center, "Generation Gap."

who agree with that idea.[47] No poll has been conducted with only Gen Z respondents to determine their attitudes toward diplomacy versus military intervention; however, a 2018 study by the Chicago Council on Global Affairs concluded every generation is consistently less in favor of military intervention than their parent's generation.[48]

This means it is reasonable for one to expect Generation Zers to have similar attitudes to Millennials regarding a preference for diplomacy over military action. Those Gen Zers I talked to who do support foreign interventions are usually young foreign policy hawks who are hyper-fixated on Bush-era foreign influence operations. Many of these hawks care deeply about human rights and view it as the United States' duty to intervene in matters of human rights abuse overseas.

***

Gen Zers watched their fathers, brothers, sisters, mothers, and family friends get shipped off to the Middle East, making them less likely to support military action overseas. Most of the people I interviewed for this book recalled their first political memory as something happening in the tail end of the Bush Era or the very beginning of the Obama era. Jacob Pride, a Democrat from Pennsylvania, said his first political memory was his father's deployment to Afghanistan. He wanted to understand why his father was sent overseas and

47 Ibid.
48 Trevor Thrall, Dina Smeltz, Erik Goepner, Will Ruger, and Craig Kafura, "The Clash of Generations? Intergenerational Change and American Foreign Policy Views," *The Chicago Council on Global Affairs*, June 25, 2018.

who got to make that decision. When Pride learned of Bush's role as commander-in-chief, he asked one of his teachers if the president could be fired. Pride said his father's deployment made him more progressive in that it "didn't make me an anti-interventionist, but it did make me more anti-conflict and at least apprehensive about war."

Every Gen Zer who was interviewed for this book was too young to have their own clear recollection of the events that unfolded on 9/11 but old enough to understand its significance in the context of American history and its political implications. Ryan Moore, a Libertarian from North Carolina, said his earliest political memory was half-watching the news with his parents while clips of Bush and discussions about the Iraq War were being aired. Moore also recalls his neighbor going to fight in the war in Afghanistan. Tyler Gardner, president of the Kent State College Democrats, recalls the incident when Iraqi reporter Muntadhar al-Zaidi threw two shoes at President George W. Bush as his first political memory. Travis Legault, a Democrat from California, was around four and a half years old at the time that 9/11 happened and was the only Gen Zer I spoke to who had a vague memory of the day.

Around the ages of seven or eight, Gen Zers were starting to become more curious about the government and the American political system. When I was around that age, I recall seeing gold ribbons tied on trees in support of American troops in my hometown and sending care packages to soldiers fighting overseas through Operation Shoebox. While Gen Zers were too young to truly understand what was happening, the War on Terror was being waged in the background of their childhood.

The events of 9/11 and the War on Terror seems to bear more significance for Gen Zers who, like myself, grew up in communities that were close in proximity to New York City and had large populations of commuters. This also applies to Gen Zers who grew up in and around Arlington, Virginia by the Pentagon and near Shanksville, Pennsylvania, where the fourth plane crashed into a field. People in these areas were more likely to tell me about attachments to people who passed away, were injured in, or barely escaped the attacks.

***

For me, the mere proximity to New York City alone prompts an emotional attachment to the day. I cry every year on 9/11. I read chilling accounts from that day: near misses, miraculous escapes, heroic rescues. I mourn the victims who I never knew and will never forget, a skyline I do not remember, and an America I never knew. I grieve for the soldiers who never came home, the wounded warriors, and the families who lost mothers, fathers, sons, and daughters. I've seen the bent steel outside of my town's city hall, choked back tears across the dining table from a first responder recounting that tragic September day.

I've participated in moments of silence at the exact times the planes hit the towers, visited the Pentagon memorial, and prayed under the stained-glass depiction of the Twin Towers in my university's chapel. I have prayed at each of the benches on my university's campus dedicated in memory of

9/11 victims, unable to shake the feeling my life is inextricably linked to those cut far too short. I cannot bear to bring myself to visit Ground Zero because I can never associate that space with anything other than mass tragedy and sheer terror. It overwhelms me to think about stepping foot on the site where so many innocent Americans had their lives taken away by an act of terrorism. Gen Zers, although most were too young to remember 9/11 or were born after that tragic day, maintain attachments to those events and their aftermath.

4

MEDIA LITERACY

———

TikTok, Twitter, Instagram, Facebook, Snapchat, LinkedIn, YouTube, Discord, and Twitch. Social media has changed the way people interact with one another, learn about different topics, entertain themselves, purchase items, conduct professional networking, and hold discussions. The World Wide Web is an exciting and terrifying place, capable of spreading truth and lies, inspiring good and evil, and starting political and social movements. Generation Z were born with the world at their fingertips, having been exposed to technology from a very young age. Their natural predisposition toward utilizing social media allows them to organize and mobilize through digital platforms with ease. The politicians currently in power in Washington have struggled to effectively conduct oversight on and regulate social media platforms, giving big tech companies wide-ranging discretion to moderate content on their platforms as they choose. Looking forward, regulating big tech and developing a deep understanding of social media as a double-edged sword capable of good and evil will be the major task of the next generation of American leaders.

Gen Zers are digital natives, meaning they do not know what life without access to technology is like. According to Pew Research Center, 45 percent of Gen Zers say they are online "almost constantly," meaning they are rapidly consuming information at a pace unimaginable for every previous generation.[49] Sites like Twitter and Reddit facilitate conversations between Gen Zers and people from all corners of the world. It's through these sites that I easily found dozens of politically active Gen Zers across America to interview for this book.

The internet is the greatest tool for organization and mobilization this world has ever seen. As digital natives, Gen Z knows how to use it better than anyone else. Gen Z's social media prowess is revolutionary in a way that they use it to challenge traditional bastions of power. Through social media sites, Gen Zers build large audiences who they can mobilize, share political opinions with, disseminate political information through, and engage in political discourse with. These online communities have the ability to influence the national political conversation, and no one understands how to employ them better than Gen Zers. For America's young activists, technology gives them the chance to play offense.

***

From the minute President Donald Trump scheduled his big comeback rally in Tulsa, Oklahoma, the event was destined for disaster. Cases of COVID-19 were rising in Tulsa, Oklahoma, and a crowded rally could quickly turn into a

---

49 Kim Parker and Ruth Igielnik, "On the Cusp of Adulthood and Facing an Uncertain Future: What We Know about Gen Z So Far," *Pew Research Center*, May 14, 2020.

super-spreader event.[50] The rally was originally scheduled for June 19, 2020, also known as Juneteenth.[51] Juneteenth garnered increased attention in 2020 amid the Black Lives Matter protests, with many cities and employers recognizing it as a holiday. Juneteenth commemorates the day General Granger of the Union army announced all slaves held in Texas were free. The location of the rally only exacerbated criticism of Trump's decision to hold the rally. Tulsa, Oklahoma was the site of what is largely regarded as the worst episode of racial violence in the history of the United States. In the Tulsa Race Massacre of 1921, white mobs killed Black men while looting and burning their houses and businesses in the Greenwood district, once known as "Black Wall Street."[52] The date of the rally coupled with the location during a moment of heightened racial tension was seen widely as an intentional signal of disrespect to the Black community.

Young people on Twitter and TikTok sprang into action to undermine the rally. Collectives of TikTok teens and Twitter stan accounts (also known as celebrity fan accounts) for K-Pop (Korean pop) groups launched campaigns that encouraged users to reserve tickets to Trump's rally. Their goal? Create a stadium full of empty seats. They raised the Trump campaign's attendance expectations so high that top-ranking officials made the mistake of prematurely announcing

---

50 The Associated Press, "Trump Picks Tulsa on Juneteenth for Return to Rallies," *NBC News*, published June 10, 2020.

51 Ibid.

52 Chris M. Messer, Thomas E. Shriver, and Alison E. Adams, "The Destruction of Black Wall Street: Tulsa's 1921 Riot and the Eradication of Accumulated Wealth," *Am J Econ Sociol* 77, no. 3-4 (May-September 2018): 789-819.

that one million people had RSVP'd to the event.[53] This was not the first time Trump's critics had attempted to thwart his rallies by reserving seats, but it was the most successful. Trump's advance team was anticipating a record-shattering number of supporters to turn out in Tulsa. In addition to the almost twenty-thousand-seat arena where the rally was being held, Trump's camp created an outdoor stage and standing area to accommodate a crowd in the tens to hundreds of thousands.[54] Trump was scheduled to deliver a second speech to what his team assured him would be a rapturous sea of MAGA hat-wearing fans. The outdoor stage was dismantled before the rally even started.

The poor attendance at the Tulsa rally is one example of the way Trump's campaign underestimated the ability of Gen Zers to mobilize in opposition to him. Photos from journalists inside the arena showed rows upon rows of empty seats. Just over six thousand people watched Donald Trump deliver a rambling, practically incoherent, speech to a measly flock of middle-aged Oklahoma-natives in MAGA hats, most of them refusing to wear masks.[55] Even though the TikTok teens had raised expectations to astronomical levels, there is no evidence they barred people from attending the event.

Seats are issued on a first-come, first-serve basis, and despite claims from Trump's advisors that protestors had blocked the entrance, reporters at the scene say no one was turned

53   Taylor Lorenz, Kellen Browning, and Sheera Frenkel, "TikTok Teens and K-Pop Stans Say They Sank Trump Rally," *The New York Times*, June 21, 2020.

54   Ibid.

55   Ibid.

away or unable to enter. The almost incomprehensibly high number of RSVPs did likely deter the attendance of those concerned about the pandemic. The anticipated crowd of hundreds of thousands juxtaposed with the cancellation of Trump's outdoor event were extremely embarrassing for the campaign. It was a massive failure that could have been prevented if Trump's campaign had been in touch with tech-savvy teens. Youth outreach has been a major blind spot for the Trump campaign and their unwillingness to understand teens as a major mobilizing force against Trump contributed to this major campaign rally faux pas.

Politicians no longer rely on television ads to win over voters. Instead, they bank on digital ads. Presidential candidate Mike Bloomberg paid popular meme accounts on Instagram to display ads for his campaign to reach Gen Z voters.[56] In his 2018 Senate Campaign, Beto O'Rourke went live on Instagram almost every single day, even while driving his car.[57] Senator Ed Markey has attracted a cult-like following on Twitter by sharing memes and playing into internet trends.[58] My home state of New Jersey has garnered a loyal Twitter and Instagram following by using slang and meme formats to increase engagement with their content.[59] It makes a state government seem relatable; not to mention, their content is actually funny.

56 Kaitlyn Tiffany, "You Can't Buy Memes," *The Atlantic*, February 28, 2020.

57 Dan Soloman, "Beto O'Rourke's Endless Livestream," *Texas Monthly*, November 12, 2018.

58 Kara Voght, "The Memeable Mr. Markey," *Mother Jones*, August 26, 2020.

59 Andrew Marantz, "How New Jersey's Twitter Found Its 'Big State Energy,'" *The New Yorker*, published January 20, 2020.

Social media content is at its best when it is employed to establish personal connections between the user and the audience. Trump's 2016 victory was in large thanks to the millions that his campaign spent on Facebook advertisements.[60] Special Counsel Robert Mueller discovered Trump also received some help from foreign troll farms and ads purchased by the internet Research Agency in Russia.[61]

Trump's personal social media functioned as a megaphone that he periodically shouted threats into. In the end, he did more to alienate potential supporters, inflame political divisions, and incite violence through his social media accounts than to advance his political agenda and expand his base. Politicians need to learn to make relatable content that makes them approachable to their constituents and advances their professional interests. Campaign officials also need to weaponize it as a means of mobilizing and educating voters while maintaining open lines of dialogue between them and the candidate.

TikTok has not yet been utilized by many politicians to engage with young voters. For some politicians, this is likely due to the very valid security concerns they have about TikTok's ties to the Chinese government. One politician, Senator Jon Ossoff, successfully utilized the platform to reach thousands of Gen Zers in his campaign for a Georgia

---

60 Christine B. Williams, and Girish J. "Jeff" Gulati, "Digital Advertising Expenditures in the 2016 Presidential Election," *Social Science Computer Review* 36, no. 4 (August 2018): 406–21.

61 Robert S. Mueller III, *The Mueller Report*, (Washington D.C.: U.S. Department of Justice, 2019), 24-26.

Senate seat. Important political discussions are happening on the platform.

Gen Zers use the internet to organize mass protests and demonstrations because it is the fastest way to share information with their generational peers. It also gives them a platform to inform their generational peers about foundational political theory books, from De Tocqueville to Locke. Teachers and professors have utilized the platform to educate teens and young adults about American history, international relations theory, and electoral politics. Gen Zers are digital natives and thus are naturally adept at utilizing social media as a tool to further their social and political agendas. This is unique to Gen Z not just because of their nativism, but because of their innate ability to build coalitions through unexpected avenues.

Gen Zers have been unable to assert power through traditional media and political structures so they have turned to new forms of media. Their penchant for creativity and messaging has made social media the perfect platform for their political discourse. Digital nativism does not preclude politicians from older generations from understanding the fundamental aspects of social media like the role that algorithms, curation/personalization, advertisements, third party trackers, and engagement play on the platforms. Their lack of digital nativism creates a hurdle for them in that older Americans must contend with a technological learning curve. The slow progression of technological skills for older politicians is worth enduring to familiarize themselves with a rapidly changing social and political environment rooted in the expansion of social media.

Legacy media is no longer able to act alone in their capacity as gatekeepers for news and agenda-setters for governmental institutions. Viral memes and Twitter trends have just as much capacity to ignite a social movement as a segment on CNN. Teens form political collectives on sites like TikTok to debate politics and spread newsworthy information to fellow American teenagers. Memes serve as political commentary and allow users to spread damaging information about politicians that reach an audience of millions. Instagram stories feature infographics encouraging teens to sign petitions and call their government representatives. As seen in the Black Lives Matter movement, social media can be used to counter narratives provided by the police and the mainstream media. A smartphone has become a tool to ensure accountability and to amplify marginalized voices.

***

At the intersection of social media and politics lies a new challenge the United States government must act on promptly. Gen Z knows how to weaponize social media to achieve their own goals. That means they also know how social media can be weaponized to achieve evil ends. Generation Z came of age during the rise of cyberbullying and have grown up in the age of doxing, cybercrime, and catfishing. Many Gen Zers have participated in this "evil" side of social media as not all of them use these platforms in a manner that is inherently good. The platforms many users employ to spearhead social justice initiatives, inform themselves, and educate others are also many of the same platforms used to organize an insurrection against the United States government on January 6, 2021. Social media sites have also been utilized by white supremacists and neo-Nazis to communicate with each other and radicalize other users. In recognition of this, for the sake of our democracy's health, I predict there is a reckoning coming for big tech companies.

Gen Zers know better than anyone that social media companies themselves need oversight and regulation due to their reluctance to police user behavior. Currently, there is little regulation of digital political advertising and native disinformation content (also known as "fake news"). This has facilitated an increase in political polarization and the ability of certain actors to manipulate users' political beliefs. This was evidenced in the Mueller report findings which outlined a network of hackers and foreign actors based in Russia that sowed disinformation in the lead-up to the 2016 presidential election.[62]

Although these actors were able to be prosecuted under the Foreign Agent Registration Act, there is little regulation of domestic actors who wage digital disinformation campaigns. There are also few regulations addressing misuse of data collection, resulting in scandals like Cambridge Analytica wherein data was unwillingly collected from users under false pretenses and sold to advisors on political campaigns, including Donald Trump's.[63] Regulating big tech will be the major political challenge of the next decade.

62 Mueller, *The Mueller Report*, 4-11.
63 Matthew Rosenberg, Nicholas Confessore, and Carole Cadwalladr, "How Trump Consultants Exploited the Facebook Data of Millions," *The New York Times,* March 17, 2018.

As of January 8, 2021, Donald Trump has been permanently banned from Twitter, Facebook, and Instagram.[64] Other platforms, ranging from Snapchat to Pinterest, have also followed suit.[65] Kicking a world leader off of social media is not a decision taken lightly by the platforms. It speaks to the severity of the democratic crisis facilitated by the president's own rhetoric. The decision has also ignited debates around the role of big tech and the limitations that should be placed on their abilities to moderate online discourse.

***

As private companies, platforms like Facebook and Twitter are not required to protect the First Amendment right of freedom of speech. They are also shielded by Section 230 of the Communications Decency Act which protects them from being held liable for content posted by users and gives them broad powers to moderate content as they see fit. Section 230 has become a lightning rod for political debate, seen by both parties as an obstacle to ensuring accountability for big tech companies. This ire is misguided. Seeing as Section 230 provides these companies with protection from liability for content posted on their respective platforms, its full repeal would likely result in stricter moderation of content to prevent an onslaught of lawsuits.

"The law runs way behind on these things," said Roger McNamee, an early investor in Facebook, "but what I know is the current situation exists not for the protection of users,

---

64   Kate Conger and Mike Isaac, "Twitter Permanently Bans Trump, Capping Online Revolt," *The New York Times,* January 10, 2020.

65   Ibid.

but for the protection of the rights and privileges of these gigantic, incredibly wealthy companies."[66] If politicians are concerned about the unequal application of rules and the wide-ranging discretion that tech companies have to suspend or delete accounts, place disclaimers on content, and remove photos and videos, reforming Section 230 is a place to start but completely repealing it would be antithetical to their mission.

In the near future, platforms like Facebook and Twitter are likely to face increasing regulations pertaining to disclaimers for political advertisements and incendiary rhetoric on their platforms. This was famously pointed out by Senator Elizabeth Warren who ran a false ad on Facebook for her presidential campaign to point out the flaws in Facebook's advertising guidelines. Users are constantly being fed inaccurate information and the algorithms for these social media sites are reinforcing their pre-existing political beliefs. This is an existential threat to our democracy.

Former FEC Chairman, Ann Ravel, told me in an interview for my legal research paper on digital political advertising that Facebook needs to be "a consistent mediator," meaning it cannot simply pick and choose which content to fact-check. Fact-check one advertisement, fact-check all of them. Dr. Shoshana Zuboff, Professor Emeritus at Harvard Business School and author of *The Age of Surveillance Capitalism,* warned social media companies trade in human futures and bet on creating predictable behavioral changes in users.

---

66   *The Social Dilemma,* directed by Jeff Orlowski, written by Davis Coombe, Vickie Curtis, and Jeff Orlowski, featuring Tristan Harris Produced by Exposure Labs. (Los Gatos, CA: Netflix, 2020).

Zuboff said of this profit model, "These markets undermine democracy, and they undermine freedom, and they should be outlawed."[67]

In a market where users gain clout and make profit off of misinformation, algorithms can facilitate radicalization and stoke political divisions. The online spread of QAnon, Pizzagate, and other conspiracies revolving around the political elite class and their popularity among many Trump supporters, including those who stormed the Capitol on January 6, 2021, is just one example of how these platforms are reaching a breaking point in terms of what content they are comfortable hosting.

The problem is many politicians in office right now do not understand the extent of the danger stemming from these platforms because some of them do not even understand how to use them or how they are operated. While the lack of digital nativism is a hurdle for accessibility and ease of use, it is not insurmountable. The lack of knowledge on behalf of older members of the government as it relates to regulating digital platforms is so stark that one cannot help but think it is the product of a refusal to engage with them on even the most basic level.

In an infamous exchange during a joint hearing of the Senate Judiciary and Commerce, Science, and Transportation committees, Sen. Orrin Hatch (R-UT) asked Facebook CEO Mark Zuckerberg, "If [a version of Facebook will always be free] how do you sustain a business model in which users don't

---

67   Ibid.

pay for your service?"[68] Zuckerberg, clearly attempting to hold back a laugh, smugly responded, "Senator, we run ads."[69] Politicians need to understand the subjects of regulation to create effective legislation. Otherwise, these private platforms will lack the oversight necessary to prevent evil actors from further abusing them without repercussions.

Politicians have to embrace the digital revolution as Millennials and Gen Zers begin to compose a larger share of the American electorate. These same politicians must also recognize the need for increased regulation of social media platforms. Digital disinformation is the most pressing threat to the stability of our democracy and must be treated as such. Gen Z knows the internet is capable of creating good in the world, but it also has an extremely dark side. It will be the task of our generation to expose that and to force politicians to engage in critical dialogue about the necessity to combat those evils.

---

68   Emily Stewart, "Lawmakers Seem Confused about What Facebook Does-
      and How They Do It," *Vox*, April 10, 2018.
69   Ibid.

PART III

IDENTITIEZ

5

GEN Z AND RACE

The year is 2008. Mia Arrington, at just seven years old, is standing on her tiptoes attempting to see over the heads of the hundreds of people packed into the Columbia Metropolitan Convention Center. Her whole family had made the trip from Maryland down to South Carolina to canvass during the week leading up to the state's presidential primary. Now, as results began to trickle in, Mia was practically buzzing with excitement as the primary night rally exploded with energy. She listened to a rousing, triumphant speech with rapt attention, mesmerized by the spectacle unfolding in front of her.

Suddenly, as the event began to wind down and she realized how distant her family was from the stage, she burst into tears. That's when Mia's sister grabbed her by the hand and began forcefully snaking her way through the crowd filled with raucous supporters; she was not going to let this opportunity pass them by. Mia's sobs echoed through the crowd as the horde of people gradually parted to let them through. "Baby, why are you crying?" Mia found herself in the arms of the man who had just uttered those words, her tearful eyes regaining their focus as she locked eyes with the man she had been so desperate to meet: Barack Obama.

***

I asked dozens of Generation Zers what their first political memory was. Some cited news coverage of the Iraq War, others the 2004 and 2016 elections. Approximately half of the respondents replied it was watching the electoral victory or inauguration of President Barack Obama, the first Black man to assume the office of the presidency. It was a watershed moment in American politics and a key event in the political socialization of Gen Zers. The idea that a Black man who started his political career as a community organizer in the Southside of Chicago could become president depicts a uniquely American tale of triumph in the face of systemic oppression.

This chapter will explore how Obama's electoral victories in 2008 and 2012 along with the rise of birtherism, racist rhetoric, and public instances of police brutality in the 2010s molded the political attitudes of Gen Zers. Gen Zers began to comprehend the American political system, in all of its imperfection, through the lens of the Obama administration and the corresponding political climate. The Black Lives Matter movement also played a significant role in Generation Z's political socialization, beginning with the murder of Trayvon Martin in 2012. Gen Zers' exposure to conversations that revolved around the intersection of race, politics, and social justice at a young age positioned racial justice as a salient issue for them.

The political socialization of Gen Z occurred in the context of a greater, nationwide discourse surrounding the murders of unarmed Black men at the hands of policemen and vigilantes. This discourse was happening not just in mass media but in the walls of their own homes, forcing Generation Z to think critically about race. Additionally, Gen Z's status as the most racially diverse generation in American history has made racial justice a priority across partisan lines.[70] These race-related events and the national conversations around them predisposed Gen Zers to be sympathetic toward policy proposals that attempt to remedy racial disparities in the United States. In their roles as voters and future leaders, Gen Zers see racial equality as a key issue. Recognizing this is central to the electoral viability of both major parties over the next two decades.

***

In hindsight, many Gen Zers are now able to grasp the reality of the political, social, and racial revolution that was Obama's election in 2008. Ethan Block, from central New Jersey, said of Obama's victory: "I had no understanding of racism as a seven-year-old white kid. I wish I understood the magnitude of [Obama's election] at the time." This was the first election where Gen Zers were cognizant of the event they were bearing witness to, yet they were still too young to understand the depth of its historical importance. In their eyes, still clouded by the innocence of youth which precluded them

---

70 Kim Parker and Ruth Igielnik, "On the Cusp of Adulthood and Facing an Uncertain Future: What We Know about Gen Z So Far," *Pew Research Center*, May 14, 2020.

from understanding the political context of the moment, a presidential election was cause for excitement.

Interviewees relayed vivid memories of mock elections in their elementary schools and heading to the polls with their parents to watch them vote for the first time. They also spoke of the excitement of having a TV rolled into their respective classrooms, which they and their classmates huddled around to watch the first Black president's Inauguration. Ryan Wolfe, a Democrat from Iowa, recalled getting to caucus for Obama with his mother: "The energy in the room was electric at that moment. I knew then that [politics] was something I was interested in studying really for the rest of my life." That experience made Wolfe a staunch Obama supporter. When his school held a mock election just days before the 2008 election, Wolfe launched into organizer mode: "I decided on my own that I would campaign for Obama at my school." Obama won that mock election in Wolfe's small, private Catholic elementary school in Iowa. Obama went on to win the state of Iowa's seven electoral votes and, of course, the 2008 presidential election.

Keith Nagy, national political affairs director for the College Democrats of America, had a similar experience in his elementary school's 2008 mock election. Nagy explained, "I remember being one of the few Obama voters because I am from rural Kansas, so it is a very conservative atmosphere, and I definitely felt like the election of Barack Obama was a moment where I thought that the country was finally changing for the better." On election night in November 2008, Nagy and his parents recorded the CNN coverage. They kept it on their television for a long time, and Nagy would frequently rewatch the program to relive the excitement of that night. He watched it so often he "was able to quote various aspects of the commentary that night." Nagy has vivid memories of the moment when Obama was declared the victor. He also remembers "all the people in Grant Park cheering and waving the American flag." Nagy memorized parts of the speech Obama gave that fateful November night; it had clearly struck a chord deep inside of him.

Generation Z's introduction to American politics was a message of hope and change that propelled the first Black president into office. Elder Gen Zers clung onto Obama's message and his vision for a more just, inclusive America. For young, Black Americans, the importance of Obama's election was immediately apparent. Mia Arrington, a Black woman from Maryland, comes from a family of Democratic politicians and has interned in the House of Representatives and the Senate. Arrington had been making calls and knocking on doors for Obama at just seven years old before she met the man himself in South Carolina. Hailing from a predominantly Black suburb of DC in Maryland, Mia acknowledged she had been "living in a bubble where there is a lot of affluent Black people and our government was reflective of that." In Obama, Mia saw the federal government could represent the growing Black population in the United States.

Michelle Charles, a Black woman from North Carolina, recalled her parents making her and her siblings watch the election night coverage in 2008. At nine years old, Charles was reaching the age where she was becoming politically aware; that coupled with the excitement of the election of the first Black president instantly made her interested in politics.

On inauguration day, Michelle's school was not planning to convene the students to watch Obama take the oath of office. In a strange twist of fate, it snowed in North Carolina on January 20, 2009, and Michelle got to watch Barack Obama become the forty-fourth president of the United States of America; she says it was "meant to be."

Seeing a Black man assume the office of the presidency served as a critical moment in the political socialization of Gen Zers, especially young Black Americans. Noah Fenstermacher, a Black man from Pennsylvania, said "most of [the Rebuilding Generation] became more aware around 2008 and because it was the first Black president, it sparked a more visceral reaction."

Obama's election was both important as a historic moment for America and as a milestone in the Rebuilding Generation's political awareness. Fenstermacher noted that while Obama's election provided hope for young Black Americans like himself, the reaction of more conservative Americans who "were uncomfortable with the idea of the first Black president in the Oval Office...opens your eyes to the idea that some people make judgments about you based on the color of your skin." This forced Gen Zers to engage in critical thinking revolving around the dual reality of a Black man assuming the highest office in the country and the racism that pervaded American society, which they were beginning to be exposed to in their pre-teen years. The oldest members of Gen Z were thirteen years old when Obama first took the oath of office, a crucial age when belief systems are beginning to take shape. This resulted in an extraordinary interest in racial justice issues for many young Americans.

As Obama continued his tenure in office, racism continued to rear its ugly head in American political discourse. First there were birtherism conspiracy theories falsely alleging Obama was actually a Muslim who was born in Kenya and then there were the increased media coverage of brutal murders of young black men at the hands of police.[71] The eldest members of Generation Z approached a formative period for their political and racial consciousness heading into their teenage years in the early-to-mid-2010s. They had to reconcile the hope of Barack Obama with a different, darker side of the American experience: racism.

***

On February 26, 2012, seventeen-year-old Trayvon Martin, an unarmed young Black man, was shot by George Zimmerman in Sanford, Florida while on his way back to a family member's townhouse from a 7/11.[72] In the subsequent national outcry over Martin's death and Zimmerman's acquittal, the Black Lives Matter movement was born.[73] Martin's death will be regarded as a cultural and political flashpoint in American history, especially in the minds of Generation Z. The pre-teens that became politically conscious and socially aware while watching coverage of Martin's death are now the ones protesting in the streets and bringing their beliefs about racial justice to the voting booth.

---

71 Ben Smith and Byron Tau, "Birtherism: Where It All Began," *Politico*, April 22, 2011.

72 Miami Herald Staff, "A Look at What Happened the Night Trayvon Martin Died," *The Tampa Bay Times*, July 6, 2012.

73 Karen Grigsby Bates, "A Look Back at Trayvon Martin's Death, and the Movement It Inspired," *NPR*, July 31, 2018.

Black Lives Matter is not just a protest movement; it's a political, cultural, and social revolution that has transformed the political attitudes of American voters. This is especially true for young, Black Americans who regard Martin's murder as a key turning point in their political awakening. Michelle Charles, a Black woman from North Carolina, named Martin's murder as a definitive event in the formation of her political identity. As Charles spoke, I could hear the residual frustration in her voice as she recalled the Martin case as "the first time I realized the innate unfairness of the justice system." Charles said it made her realize "I need to be dialed into issues of racial justice. It's my life on the line. It's my dad's life, my brother's life, my mom's life."

Michelle was just thirteen years old when Martin was murdered. In the images of him that flashed across the television screen, she did not see a stranger; Michelle saw herself and her loved ones. That personal connection to Martin and the bitter taste of injustice that has been consistently reinforced by Michelle's own experiences with racism and microaggression, as well as the continued murder of young Black men and black trans women, has cemented a passion for racial justice at the center of Charles' political identity. She is not the only one who still carries the pain of Martin's death in her heart. Mia Arrington, a Black woman from Maryland, says of the personal grief that accompanied Martin's death, "I've carried that with me my entire life." For young, Black Americans, Martin's murder was personal. It was a loss not just of a young man, but for many, their innocence.

Being aware of widespread racial violence at such a young age, as well as growing up as part of the most diverse generation in American history, has had a profound impact on Gen Z. In the midst of the Black Lives Matter movement they have come to realize that, as Ethan Block put it, "You can't just not be racist; you have to be anti-racist." Black Lives Matter has been misconstrued by some as a Black supremacy movement instead of its true purpose as an inclusive public influence campaign against systemic racism. Mia Arrington said being a part of the Black Lives Matter movement "means you don't stand for letting people lose their lives because of racist beliefs." Arrington explains a major part of that belief is recognizing that "systemic racism does not protect Black lives."

The broadness of the movement and the lack of a central leadership structure has created a sense of confusion about the movement's protest methods, beliefs, and demands. Noah Fenstermacher said one of the negative effects of the Black Lives Matter movement has been "some people claim[ing] to do something to represent the whole movement when they are actually uneducated and ignorant. I don't want their views to be conflated with my own because we are claiming to be a part of the same movement." At the center of the Black Lives Matter movement is the deep-rooted sentiment that Black people's lives are *just as valuable* as white people's lives and deserved to be recognized as such. It is a way for them to assert their worth in the face of the intergenerational trauma caused by routine violence against Black Americans. The movement is also a way for Black people to build multi-racial coalitions with allies who will help advance the cause of racial equality.

***

For non-Black people of color in Generation Z, the Black Lives Matter movement has also served as a wake-up call. Krissie Palomo, a young Latina woman from Texas, explained, "As a person of color, over this past year, learning how to be an ally to my Black counterparts has definitely been life changing. I've noticed I was guilty of having microaggressions in my daily life, something that I didn't even notice, and it's something that I had to hold myself accountable for." Palomo mentioned how fortunate she is to be surrounded by young, Black activists who are at the forefront of the Black Lives Matter movement in her community. She was grateful they took the time to educate her about racial injustice, microaggressions, and the Black experience; however, she noted the onus is not on Black people to educate white people and non-Black people of color.

For non-Black Gen Zers, the work of being anti-racist is as much about self-reflection and education as it is about external action. Palomo called for other members of her generation to "take the time to be uncomfortable with themselves. Just sit down and look at what they do in their daily lives that may be considered microaggressions even if they do not even notice it." After the murder of George Floyd in May of 2020, renewed interest in the Black Lives Matter movement sparked even more Gen Zers, including young white people, to become outspoken about racial justice issues. Ryan Wolfe explained that "white people are often not given the language to deal with talking about racism," but through anti-racism media and content related to the Black Lives Matter movement, Wolfe believes "we are being exposed to more new ideas and creating a cohesive generational narrative around racial justice." Wolfe's point brings up another side of political socialization: lack of exposure to adequate rhetorical frameworks for policy-based discussions.

Many Americans are barred from engaging in constructive political discourse if they do not have knowledge of the specific language that is employed in that subject area. This creates a disconnect when people want to engage in the discourse surrounding the issue of racial injustice, but do not have the language to do so. As they attempt to engage in tough, often uncomfortable, conversations about race in America, many white people are reluctant because they're afraid they will say the wrong thing. In order to have these conversations, it is imperative non-Black Americans familiarize themselves with anti-racist work and the rhetoric of racial justice movements. That work begins in the communities in which they are raised and should be introduced at the start of their education.

***

With the spotlight on police brutality and racial justice issues, many young white people are finding the communities they live in are not the havens they once believed them to be. Ethan Block, a young white man, explained, "We like to think because we are northern, liberal towns that didn't vote for Trump we are not racist." At the time that I spoke to him, Block's town of Hopewell Valley was reconciling with revelations of racial harassment within the town's police department. This is representative of a larger reckoning at hand where Americans are taking long, hard looks at institutions intrinsically tied to systemic racism, including their local police departments.

Among these reckonings, there have been calls to restructure police departments and rethink their role in American communities. The "defund the police" movement, popularized in 2020, advocates for a reallocation of public safety resources to encourage alternative responses to incident reports (enlisting the help of social workers and mental health professionals) and investment in other public sectors like education, infrastructure, and public health.[74] The "defund the police" movement gained momentum after the murder of George Floyd by officers from the Minneapolis police department.[75] Floyd's murder served as a wake-up call for activists in the Black Lives Matter movement who wanted to debate the role that police play (and the power they hold) in American society. The Black Lives Matter movement is a reaction to the racial injustice that has been present in America for centuries. The recent string of highly publicized murders of Black men are the most recent chapter in an epidemic of violence against Black people in America.

*＊＊

Generation Z is the most racially and ethnically diverse generation in American history, with just over half of the generation identifying as non-Hispanic White.[76] The voice of people of color in America has never been louder. The unjust murder of Black people at the hands of police is inextricably

---

74 Farah Stockman and John Eligon, "Cities Ask if It's Time to Defund Police and 'Reimagine' Public Safety," *The New York Times*, June 5, 2020.

75 Ibid.

76 Amanda Barroso, "Gen Z Eligible Voters Reflect the Growing Racial and Ethnic Diversity of U.S. Electorate," *Pew Research Center*, September 23, 2020.

linked to the collective political identity of Gen Z. Beliefs about the treatment of Black people in America transcends partisanship for this generation in a way that sets them apart from all other generational cohorts.[77] In the faces of the Black men and women killed at the hands of the police, Gen Z sees friends, family members, classmates, co-workers, partners, and teammates.

While many suburban American neighborhoods remain as relics of white flight and redlining, America is becoming increasingly aware of the opportunity gaps between Black and white citizens. Increasing racial diversity in America mandates the two major parties address issues of racial injustice including police brutality, mass incarceration, the school-to-prison pipeline, and de-facto segregation if they want to be relevant to the American electorate in the decades to come. In America's post-crisis rebuilding period in the mid to late 2020s, creating a more inclusive system of governance that addresses the critical gaps in opportunity between Black and white people will be paramount.

Increasing the representation of Black people in local, state, and federal government and acknowledging the concerns of Black voters is the first step toward addressing racial inequality. It is Black voters who propelled Barack Obama to the presidency, and it was low turnout among Black voters that barred Hillary Clinton from the highest office in the nation.[78]

---

77 Parker and Igelnik, "On the Cusp of Adulthood."

78 Andrew P. Jackson, Denyvetta Davis, and Jason Kelly Alston, "Remotivating the Black Vote: The Effect of Low-Quality Information on Black Voters in the 2016 Presidential Election and How Librarians Can Intervene," *The Library Quarterly* 87, no. 3 (July 2017), 237.

Joe Biden's victories in key swing states were propelled by his ability to rack up hundreds of thousands of votes in cities with large Black populations like Philadelphia, Detroit, Milwaukee, and Atlanta.[79]

The elections of Senators Jon Ossoff and Raphael Warnock in Georgia are one example of the way turning out voters in areas that are becoming increasingly young and diverse is changing the national political landscape.[80] Their victories, and the Democratic Senate majority, are direct results of demographic changes in Georgia, particularly Atlanta, and the efforts of grassroots organizers like Stacey Abrams and LaTosha Brown to get Black voters to the polls.[81] It is poetic that the late Civil Rights Activist Representative John Lewis' former intern, Jon Ossoff, and the man who preaches from Dr. Martin Luther King, Jr.'s former pulpit, Raphael Warnock, are heading to the Senate with the promise to pass a new Voting Rights Act.[82]

As more Black Americans run for office, it is likely systemic racial inequalities will be addressed through reforms in policy areas including but not limited to, criminal justice

---

79 John Eligon and Audra D.S. Burch,"Black Voters Helped Deliver Biden a Presidential Victory. Now What?," *The New York Times*, November 11, 2020.

80 Brian Slodysko, "Explainer: How Democrats Won Georgia's 2 Senate Runoffs," *AP News*, January 6, 2021.

81 Ibid.

82 Martin Finucane, "6 Things to Know about Rev. Raphael Warnock and Jon Ossoff," *The Boston Globe*, January 6, 2021. Reis Thebault, Michael Scherer, and Cleve R. Wootson Jr., "Raphael Warnock Wins Georgia Runoff Election against Sen. Loeffler, Lifting Democratic Hopes of Claiming Senate Majority," *The Washington Post*, January 6, 2021.

and policing, higher education, housing, healthcare, and voter enfranchisement.

By the time Generation Zers become national political leaders, there will be no way to govern without making ample room for Black and Brown voices at the table. As the most diverse generation in American history, racial equality is at the forefront of the emerging electorate's political consciousness. It is incumbent on both parties to reach out to these young people of color and to create policies with their best interest in mind. Although Black voters are not a monolith, they do have shared group interests that center around advancing their status in American society by gaining representation in financial, educational, and political institutions. Their voting habits reflect that sentiment and the next generation of American leaders, Generation Z, will embody it.

6

LATINX VOTERS

Latinos are the fastest-growing minority group in the United States and have become a key demographic within the American electorate. As members of Generation Z, America's most diverse generation, reach the age of voting eligibility, one in five of them are Latinx.[1]83 These voters made a difference in the 2020 election in key battleground states. For the first time in the nation's history, Latinx voters will constitute the second-largest racial voting bloc in the United States, surpassing Black voters' share of the electorate.[2]84 Latinx voters, especially young ones, helped decide control of the White House and the Senate in 2020.

Politicians can no longer ignore the political force that is the United States' young Latinx population. They will be a key component of every victorious national electoral coalition for the foreseeable future. The same can be said for coalitions in

---

83 Amanda Barroso, "Gen Z Eligible Voters Reflect the Growing Racial and Ethnic Diversity of U.S. Electorate," *Pew Research Center*, September 23, 2020.

84 The World Staff, "Meet the Young Latino Voters of 'Every 30 Seconds,'" *The World*, June 11, 2020.

states like Texas with a rapidly increasing young Latinx population. Both parties will need to address issues that matter to young, Latinx voters and recruit Latinx candidates for down-ballot races to maintain electoral viability. An influx of young, Latinx politicians and organizers also provides hope that the next generation of leaders will feature more people of color in positions of power. It all starts with inviting Latinx people into the political process.

In battleground states, Latinx voters have become essential to victory. Since the 2016 election, 3.6 million young Latinos have become eligible to vote.[3][85] The number of new Latinx voters in Texas, Arizona, Wisconsin, Florida, Michigan, and Pennsylvania is larger than the margin that Trump won those states by in 2016.[4][86] This is due to the fact that every thirty seconds in the United States, a young Latinx person turns eighteen years old.[5][87] Although some of them will be ineligible to vote due to their legal status, a whopping 94 percent of Gen Z Latinos will be able to cast a ballot once they turn eighteen.[6][88] This is because an overwhelming number of these Latinx voters are second or third-generation Latinx-Americans, meaning they were born in this country and are guaranteed the right to vote. Generation Z Latinos constitute almost half (47 percent) of the US-born Latinx

85   Tania Karas, "Every 30 Seconds, a Young Latino in the U.S. Turns 18. Their Votes Count More Than Ever," *High Plains Public Radio*, March 10, 2020.

86   Ibid.

87   Ibid.

88   Eileen Patten, "The Nation's Latino Population is Defined by Its Youth," *Pew Research Center*, April 20, 2016.

population.[7][89] In the next decade, the Latinx share of the US electorate will continue to grow exponentially.

Just like other racial and ethnic minority groups, Latinx voters are not a monolith. People can talk about the Latinx vote, but it is even less homogeneous than the Black vote is. Approximately two-thirds (62 percent) of eligible Latinx voters "identify with or lean toward the Democratic Party, while 34 percent affiliate with or lean to the Republican Party." [8][90] Latinx voters are also unique as they are primarily concentrated in a handful of states. Two-thirds of the Latinx electorate live in just five states: California, Texas, Florida, New York, and Arizona. Latinos also constitute a sizable share (43 percent) of the electorate in New Mexico.[9][91]

While California and New York have been reliable Democratic states in the past two decades, Texas, Florida, and Arizona pose unique opportunities for both parties to seize upon the growing Latinx population in those states. Both parties have taken notice and treated these states as critical battlegrounds in the 2020 election. The results could foretell the future of both parties in light of the rapidly changing demographics across America. Generation Z, the most diverse generation in American history, is the first indicator of what the political behavior of this majority-minority America could look like. All eyes are on young Latinx voters

89 Ibid.

90 Jens Manuel Krogstad, Ana Gonzalez-Barrera, and Christina Tamer, "Latino Democratic Voters Place High Importance on 2020 Presidential Election," *Pew Research Center,* January 17, 2020.

91 Jens Manuel Krogstad, Antonia Flores, and Mark Hugo Lopez, "Key Takeaways about Latino Voters in the 2018 Midterm Elections," *Pew Research Center,* November 9, 2018.

in Texas, a state that has quickly become a battleground in electoral contests, in a battle for the political future of the United States.

Texas is on track to become the first majority-minority state, providing a window into the political future of an increasingly diverse American population. [10][92] Texas has gone from a solidly Republican state for the past four decades to a battleground state. This transformation became apparent in 2018 as Senate candidate Beto O'Rourke coordinated a mass voter registration effort across the state leading up to the midterm elections.[11][93] Texas has historically low turnout, especially among its Latinx population, which O'Rourke set out to change in an effort to flip Texas for Democrats.

Although Latinx turnout did increase, it was not enough to deliver O'Rourke a victory; however, the surge of support for his campaign changed the way the national Democratic Party thinks about Texas. This is due in large part to Texas' Gen Z population. Youth early voting turnout in the 2018 midterms reached historic highs, increasing by almost 500 percent from the 2014 midterm elections.[12][94] This youth enthusiasm, especially among young Latinos, was the driving force behind O'Rourke's candidacy. In an analysis of the 2018 Texas Senate election results, it was found that O'Rourke performed better in counties where a high percentage of the

92 United States Census Bureau, "QuickFacts: Texas," Published July 1, 2019.

93 Nicole Narea, and Dylan Scott, "The Price—and Big Potential Payoff—of Turning Texas Blue," *Vox*, September 21, 2020.

94 Louis Jacobson, "Beto O'Rourke on Target about Scale of Democratic Surge in Texas in 2018," *PolitiFact*, June 24, 2019.

population were under the age of twenty-nine.[13]95 In these "high-youth counties," O'Rourke earned eleven percent more of the vote share on average than across all Texas counties. [14]96 This trend was even stronger in counties with high youth and Latinx populations. In the twenty Texas counties where youth made up more than 20 percent of the population and Latinx people accounted for greater than one-third of the population, O'Rourke outperformed his state-wide vote share average by 21 percentage points.[15]97

These results show young Latinx voters are the future of the Democratic Party in states like Texas and are of increasing importance to the national electorate. It is up to both parties to choose whether big investments in Texas will pay off in presidential, congressional, and down-ballot races. Texas is not a cheap state to campaign in and every dollar spent trying to turn it blue is one that is not spent in other swing states like Arizona, Florida, and North Carolina; however, turning Texas blue could expand the electoral map for Democrats and help them secure power for years to come. It would also mean building a more diverse coalition of voters that invites young Latinos to participate in the political process. It all hinges on whether or not the party decides that young Latinx voters are worth fighting (and spending big money) for.

Increasing outreach to Latinx communities, especially young voters, needs to be a major priority for both parties.

---

95 Tufts University Center for Information and Research On Civic Learning and Engagement (CIRCLE), "County by County, Youth of Color Key to Democrats in 2018," Published November 12, 2018.

96 Ibid.

97 Ibid.

Increasing turnout among young Latinx people is paramount in realizing the group's political power because politics is a virtuous cycle that rewards those who show up at the polls. If more Latinx voters go to the polls and run for office, the group will gain political clout and the issues they care about will be prioritized in the national agenda. To accomplish this, there will need to be more voter registration drives in predominantly Latinx communities, lawsuits and new legislation to dismantle systems of voter suppression efforts that target Latinx voters. Both parties will also have to actively recruit strong Latinx candidates for national, state, and local offices and create a party platform that addresses issues that matter to Latinx voters.

One issue that matters to young Latinx voters is immigration policy. Joselyn Najera, a Latina from Wichita, Kansas, pointed out that many Americans believe all Latinos come into the United States illegally. She stated, "It feels like they don't understand that it is an extremely long processes that can take many years, it's a very time-consuming process that is also very expensive. Not everyone can afford all of the expenses that come with trying to become naturalized." Najera also spoke about the demonization of undocumented people. She explained, "Most people who do end up coming here illegally simply want a better life for their loved ones. They want a better opportunity for them, oftentimes even sending money back home to help support family members. Before making such a life changing choice, there is so much thought and fear that is taken into consideration."

Najera also pointed to anti-Latino discrimination and racial justice as two other key issues for her. She referenced "the unequal treatment that many people in the Latino community face on a daily basis." Specifically, Najera pointed to the idea that Latinos "[get] discriminated against for the [simplest] actions, like speaking Spanish in public." She also spoke of the empathy she has for Black Americans, especially after the Black Lives Matter protests that occurred in the summer of 2020.

I have found Gen Z Latinx voters have been politically socialized during a time period wherein members of their racial and ethnic groups were being scapegoated and villainized (mostly by Republican politicians). They were exposed to the explicit racism of Trumpian politics toward people of Latin American descent during the peak of their political impressionability, making them more likely to identify as Democrats than older generations of Latinx Americans.[98] Like other ethnic groups, Hispanic and Latinx voters are not a monolith.[99] Many of them voted for Trump in 2020.[100] Turning out more Hispanic and Latinx voters could benefit the group and both parties in different ways.

During my research, I discovered the success of Latinx politicians on the national stage has inspired the next generation of political leaders. There is an intense enthusiasm among Gen Zers for young, Latinx politicians, namely Alexandria

98 Atiya Stokes-Brown, "The Latino Vote in the 2016 Election-Myths and Realities of the 'Trump Effect,'" In *Conventional Wisdom, Parties, and Broken Barriers in the 2016 Election*, ed. Jennifer C. Lucas, Christopher J. Galdieri, and Tauna Starbuck Sisco (Lanham, Maryland: Lexington Books, 2018), 64.

99 Geraldo L. Cadava, "How Trump Grew His Support among Latinos"," *The Atlantic*, November 9, 2020.

100 Ibid.

Ocasio-Cortez and Julian Castro. Gen Zers have been inspired by Latinx Millennial politicians and have begun to run for office. Ocasio-Cortez, a Millennial, serves as a bellwether of change in the national political arena as young Latinx people begin to claim their space in traditionally white-dominated bastions of power.

Ocasio-Cortez, or AOC, as she is commonly referred to, has permanently shaken up Capitol Hill with her progressive agenda that addresses issues that matter to young people of color and working class Americans. Gen Z Latinos are close behind as the next generation of American leaders prepares to enter power, a cohort that will be composed of more people of color. Due to how young the Latinx population in America skews, it can be said the transformations Americans are seeing in the US electorate and national political arena are just the tip of the iceberg.

Both parties need to take a long, hard look at how demographic shifts will reshape their electoral coalitions and the makeup of their caucuses over the course of the next decade. The exponential growth of the eligible-to-vote Latinx population is one extremely important factor in this demographic transformation. This is also a factor to consider when anticipating what the next generation of American leaders will look like in terms of their background, legislative priorities, and bases of support. Texas is just one state with a booming Latinx population that may serve as a case study for how young Latinx voters are changing the nature of electoral politics. As their numbers grow, so will their representation in state legislatures, Congress, and the executive branch. It is only a matter of time.

7

WOMEN AND POLITICS

———

The struggle of increasing the representation of women in government is intergenerational and bipartisan. Going all the way back to the founding of the United States of America, the country has been predominantly ruled by men. It was not until 1920 that women received the right to vote. One hundred years later, women still find themselves continually shut out of the male-dominated political arena. Relegated to the margins of major political news coverage, female politicians are discussed in relation to their spouses, children, lifestyles, wardrobes, bodies, and "ladylike" (or "unladylike") attitudes. They have attempted to enter male-dominated bastions of power but have continued to have their spotlight dimmed as the shadow of sexism is cast over them.

Women in politics have been bitterly attacked in public and private. They have been dismissed as misplaced housewives, mothers unable to balance their work and caring for their children, as well as deemed unfit to serve in high-profile public offices due to their gender. Misogynistic attacks have perpetuated a cycle wherein women are discouraged from running for office due to a lack of representation. Women who do run for office are chastised on the basis of their gender identity which further discourages female involvement in politics. Women who are elected to office are still subjected to sexist attacks. It is a cycle of discouragement. It has been over one hundred years since women gained the right to vote and were able to insert their voices into the national political debate and yet, women in politics still combat sexism on a daily basis. More women ran for office in 2020 than any other time in United States history.[101] Will they break the cycle?

As Gen Z comes of age, it is important these young women continue to reform the political arena and claim their places in male-dominated spaces. In the wake of #MeToo, a conversation has started about the power imbalances between men and women, especially in workplaces, that create toxic environments and facilitate abuse. Many male politicians, including Donald Trump, have been caught up in #MeToo scandals due to patterns of harassment and abusive behavior.[102] This conversation has only scratched the surface of the major power imbalance between an overwhelmingly male government and a majority-female population. It is a reckoning that is centuries in the making.

This chapter will look at the female politicians who Gen Zers have grown up watching in the national media. It will highlight the long shadow of sexism cast over these women's careers and the obstacles they have faced simply because of their gender. While this book tends not to look back at

---

101 Susan Davis, "Record Number of Women Run for Congress In 2020," *NPR*, June 16, 2020.

102 MJ Lee, "Trump's Accusers: 'the Forgotten' Women of the #MeToo Movement," *CNN*, July 19, 2019.

decades past, it is necessary to frame the future female leaders of Generation Z as the next fighters in an intergenerational struggle against sexism. Past political candidates have faced misogynistic attacks from the media, the public, and colleagues. The inauguration of the first female Vice President Kamala Harris on January 20, 2021 and a generation of young women ready to run for office provide hope women will gain more representation in the halls of government.

***

Congresswoman Alexandria Ocasio-Cortez was on her way to cast a vote on the morning of Monday, July 20, 2020.[103] In her signature red lipstick and high heels, she climbed the historic steps of the US Capitol on her way to the chamber that holds the House of Representatives. During her ascent, she came face-to-face with Representative Ted Yoho of Florida and Representative Roger Williams of Texas as they exited the Capitol.[104] In a now infamous tirade, Representative Yoho began accosting Ocasio-Cortez for comments she had made about the link between New York City's crime and the city's unemployment problem. "You know, You're unbelievable. You're disgusting," Yoho told Ocasio-Cortez as he wagged his finger tauntingly in her face.[105]

"Fucking bitch," Yoho muttered under his breath as he stormed off down the steps; unfortunately for him, it was

---

103 Mike Lillis, "Ocasio-Cortez Accosted by GOP Lawmaker over Remarks: 'That Kind of Confrontation Hasn't Ever Happened to Me,'" *The Hill*, July 21, 2020.

104 Ibid.

105 Ibid.

just loud enough for a reporter from *The Hill* to hear.[106] Yoho denied the comments, defending himself by saying he has been married to his wife for forty-five years and has two daughters.[107] He acted as if his proximity to women made it impossible for him to be misogynistic.

That Thursday, Ocasio-Cortez delivered a blistering speech on the House floor, decrying Yoho's behavior and subsequent excuses. "What I do have issue with is using women, wives, and daughters as shields and excuses for poor behavior," Ocasio-Cortez said.[108] She continued, "Mr. Yoho mentioned that he has a wife and two daughters. I am two years younger than Mr. Yoho's youngest daughter. I am someone's daughter too. My father, thankfully, is not alive to see how Mr. Yoho treated his daughter."[109] Ocasio-Cortez is not the first woman in politics to face misogyny, and she will not be the last.

***

Geraldine Ferraro, the first woman to be nominated for vice president, faced sexist comments about her demeanor and appearance. When she took the stage of the Democratic National Convention in 1984 to accept her nomination for vice president of the United States, legendary newscaster Tom Brokaw declared: "The first woman to be nominated for vice

106 Ibid.
107 Manu Raju, "Ocasio-Cortez Reveals New Details about Viral Incident with Rep. Ted Yoho," *CNN*, July 24, 2020.
108 David Remnick, "Alexandria Ocasio-Cortez Delivers a Lesson in Decency on the House Floor," *The New Yorker*, July 24, 2020.
109 Ibid.

president...size six."[110] In the vice presidential debate, Ferraro was asked whether the "Soviets might be tempted to take advantage of you simply because you are a woman."[111] Walter Mondale recalled a moment on the campaign trail with Ferraro: "We went down to Mississippi, and some old farmer said, 'Young lady, do you make good blueberry muffins?' And she said, 'Yes. Do you?' That was the kind of thing that she was bumping up against. She had to keep her cool. She had to be nice about it."[112] Ferraro was also negatively described as "feisty" by the political media.[113]

When a woman was finally elevated to a prominent political platform, she still faced the same outright sexism so many women have to deal with in their daily lives. Despite the power Ferraro had accumulated, her femininity remained central to her coverage in the national media. Comments about her body and other misogynistic dog-whistles followed her throughout her political career. It was extremely discouraging for women to realize they could be considered for the position that put them a heartbeat away from leadership of the free world and still be dismissed on account of their gender. It would be a lie to say we as a society have come a long way since Ferraro's candidacy.

✳✳✳

110 R.W., "Geraldine Ferraro," *The Economist*, published March 27, 2011.
111 Julia Baird, "Sarah Palin and Women Voters," *Newsweek*, September 12, 2008.
112 Walter Mondale, "Geraldine Ferraro," *TIME*, April 11, 2011.
113 R.W., "Geraldine Ferraro," *The Economist*, March 27, 2011.

When then-Alaska Governor Sarah Palin was chosen as John McCain's running mate in 2008, it shook up the entire presidential race and opened the floodgates for a barrage of sexist comments. *The Huffington Post* titled a photo gallery of Palin "Former Beauty Queen, Future VP?"[114] John Roberts, formerly of CNN and now of Fox News, wondered about Palin, "Children with Down's syndrome require an awful lot of attention. The role of vice president, it seems to me, would take up an awful lot of her time, and it raises the issue of how much time will she have to dedicate to her newborn child?"[115] The assumption was there was no way Palin could juggle the job of VP while taking care of her children. This is a double standard that has haunted women on both sides of the aisle. Due to outdated gender norms, female politicians are often viewed through the lens of their motherhood (or lack thereof). Their involvement with their children becomes a key subject of their media coverage, something that is hardly ever true for male candidates.

Media coverage unfairly focused on Palin's role as a mother and her appearance rather than debating her ability to serve as McCain's vice president. She was accused by Robin Givhan of *The Washington Post* of "dress[ing] more for pretty rather than powerful."[116] ABC's David Wright described Palin as a "young, trophy running mate."[117] Palin was objectified due

114 Beth Frerking and John F. Harris, "Clinton Aides: Palin Treatment Sexist," *Politico*, September 3, 2008.

115 Ibid.

116 Diana B. Carlin, and Kelly L. Winfrey, "Have You Come a Long Way, Baby? Hillary Clinton, Sarah Palin, and Sexism in 2008 Campaign Coverage," *Communication Studies*, Volume 60, no. 4 (September-October 2009), page 331.

117 Ibid.

to her femininity and attractive appearance while already facing an uphill battle as a little-known governor who was prone to public gaffes. Palin was by no means a perfect running mate, and it can be argued her inexperience was the nail in the coffin of McCain's 2008 campaign. However, it is no excuse for the sexist attacks that dominated media coverage of her. As scholars point out, "Palin was inexperienced and naïve much as Dan Quayle was, but no one made sexist comments about him and related his lack of qualifications to sex role stereotypes."[118] It was unfair to objectify Palin and to have her narrative tainted by the blatant misogyny of the political media.

**

Hillary Clinton, the first woman to be nominated for president by a major party, has faced sexist comments for the duration of her political career. In 2008, Chris Matthews said of Clinton, "The reason she's a U.S. senator, the reason she's a candidate for president, the reason she may be a front-runner is her husband messed around."[119] Clinton is often portrayed as a tough woman who is not conventionally attractive. Fox News' Tucker Carlson said, "When [Clinton] comes on television, I involuntarily cross my legs."[120] Her ambition is seen as threatening and unbecoming of a woman, in contrast to Palin's image as an unintimidating, traditionally feminine woman. This illustrates a phenomenon sociologists refer to as the "double bind" wherein "female leaders, much more than

118 Ibid, page 339.
119 Ibid, page 331.
120 Ibid, page 337.

their male counterparts, face the need to be warm and nice (what society traditionally expects from women), as well as competent or tough (what society traditionally expects from men and leaders)."[121]

Hillary Clinton infamously said of her professional ambitions, "I suppose I could have stayed home and baked cookies and had teas, but what I decided to do was to fulfill my profession, which I entered before my husband was in public life."[122] This comment was misconstrued as an attack on stay-at-home mothers, when really Clinton was commenting on the sexist expectations she was subjected to as First Lady. Hillary Clinton opposed the idea she could not have her own professional aspirations while being the wife of a powerful man. Sexist attacks on her only escalated as her public profile rose.

***

As former Obama advisor Valeria Jarrett pointed out, the media creates a double standard by "reporting on a woman's ambition as though the very nature of seeking political office, or any higher job for that matter is not a mission of ambition."[123] Women are not permitted to have the same level of ambition as men because gender norms have deemed it unladylike. This is a sexist double standard that prevents women

121 Wei Zheng, Ronit Kark, and Alyson Meister, "How Women Manage the Gendered Norms of Leadership," *Harvard Business Review*, November 28, 2018.

122 Kathleen Hall Jamieson, *Beyond the Double Bind: Women and Leadership*, (Oxford, England: Oxford University Press, 1995), page 28.

123 Carlin and Winfrey, "Have You Come a Long Way, Baby?" 339.

from reconciling their goals with their inherent femininity. Communication scholars Diana B. Carlin and Kelly L. Winfrey of the University of Kansas argue, "Unfortunately, because [Clinton] is 'intimidating' to some and she chose a masculine leadership style to prove she could be commander-in-chief, she was seen as fair game for sexist attacks."[124] She again faced these attacks in 2016, when Donald Trump called her "a nasty woman."[125] The "nasty" comment is not dissimilar to the way Geraldine Ferraro was described as "feisty." Again, this played on Clinton's reputation as an ambitious woman who was unafraid to play political hardball. This was an image that was seen as unladylike and reviled by major portions of the American electorate.

Some things have changed since Geraldine Ferraro took to the DNC stage to accept her nomination. Enthusiasm for female candidates is at an all-time high, yet sexism is still pervasive in American political discourse. On January 20, 2021, Kamala Harris became the first woman to serve as vice president of the United States. After Harris was announced as Joe Biden's running mate, Donald Trump called her "nasty," recycling the line of attack he used against Hillary Clinton in 2016.[126] Trump went on to call her a "madwoman" who was "condescending" and "angry."[127]

---

124 Jennifer Rubin, "Women Launch a Shot across The Media's Bow," *The Washington Post*, August 7, 2020.

125 Laura Cummings, and Jenepher Lennox Terrion, "A 'Nasty Woman': Assessing the Gendered Mediation of Hillary Clinton's Nonverbal Immediacy Cues during the 2016 U.S. Presidential Campaign," *Feminist Media Studies* 20, no. 8 (January 2020).

126 Susan Milligan, "A Historic Day, a Familiar Refrain," *U.S. News & World Report*, August 14, 2020.

127 Ibid.

The past instances of sexism against female candidates have prompted the formation of a war room to combat sexist attacks against Harris in 2020. This is a continuation of the fight that female politicians have been waging for decades in an effort to be taken seriously. There are some indications they are succeeding. A majority of Americans believe that more women running for office is a positive thing, with two-thirds of Gen Zers, Millennials, and Gen Xers agreeing.[128] This differs between men and women, with women in all generations except the Silent Generation expressing more enthusiasm for female political candidates.[129] This suggests there is a positive trend of support for female candidates running for office and could signal viability for future female-led campaigns in national and down-ballot races.

Among Gen Zers, 76 percent of young women say women running for political office is a positive thing compared to 57 percent of young men.[130] Clearly, there is still work to be done; however, young women are feeling more empowered than ever to enter male-dominated spaces. Gracie Smith, a political science student from Vermont, told me, "When more men are in power, women's rights and voices are silenced and contradicted. Without representation in higher elected offices, although not all descriptive representation contributes, women cannot expect to ever truly become equal." Still, there is a large percentage of Gen Zers who do not see increased female representation in politics as making a difference in

---

128 Kim Parker, Nikki Graf, and Ruth Igielnik, "Generation Z Looks a Lot like Millennials on Key Social and Political Issues," Pew Research Center, January 17, 2019.

129 Ibid.

130 Ibid.

society. It matters who gets a seat at the table, who gets to speak into the national microphone, and who writes the laws that govern us. Stephanie Fragoulias, a political science student from New Jersey, told me, "It is important for young girls to see their identity represented in American politics. Elected officials should be representative of the general population's demographics. Politics cannot be dominated by men."

Both physical and substantial representation in government are paramount to ensuring issues that matter to women, namely healthcare and access to higher education, are given priority in policy discussions. As Kamryn Dow, a political science student from Texas, said, "If there is a lack of representation of women in, specifically, political offices, how could legislation properly address women writ large? This also holds true for people of color. Lack of representation in elected offices most likely yields a lack of representation in legislation." It is important policy decisions are made by those who have a stake in them. Putting women in positions of power is not inherently feminist if those women are attempting to dismantle the very systems that got them there (affirmative action programs, access to reproductive care, and anti-discrimination laws). Women deserve to be in positions of power, to act in the capacity of policymakers and change-makers—not treated as objects or political pawns.

***

Generation Z will play a large role in determining how women are treated in politics going forward. It is evident Millennial politicians like Alexandria Ocasio-Cortez, are still facing sexism in their capacity as legislators. It remains to be seen whether Vice President Kamala Harris' leadership will make substantial changes in the way women are treated, although press coverage of her so far is encouraging. AOC and Harris are promising not just in respect to the female representation they offer, but also because they are women of color. Women of color have continuously struggled to climb the ladder of power due to the dual suppressive forces of racism and sexism. Their status as high-profile government leaders has inspired young women to pursue activist pathways and political leadership positions. Stephanie Fragoulias summed it up perfectly when she said, "We are living in the perfect era for young women to effectively combat sexism and become political leaders. Growing up with a female vice president in office, women will feel empowered to stand up for their own rights."

In the post-#MeToo era, it is up to the next generation of female leaders to demand they be treated with equal respect by their male counterparts. As Gracie Smith said, "Gen Z women are breaking boundaries that their Millennial and Gen X counterparts have yet to still accomplish...Gen Z's growth within the MeToo era has led us to be unwilling to accept anything short of equality in all forms." As Rebuilders carry out their destiny as team workers, it is paramount young women work together to elevate each other's voices and build a cross-racial coalition of female political thought leaders. Towering figures like Secretary Hillary Clinton, Vice President Kamala Harris, and the late Supreme Court Justice Ruth Bader Ginsburg serve as models of women in powerful positions and can be inspirations to these young women on a quest for political power.

In 2021, women are shattering the glass ceiling by successfully running for elected office. The 117th Congress features more women than any other Congress in United States history.[131] For the first time ever, the United States has a woman as their vice president.[132] Kamala Harris, who is of Jamaican and Indian descent, also became the first woman of color to serve as vice president of the United States.[133]

As gender equality and women's rights continue to be salient issues, Generation Z has the opportunity to further increase the representation of women in local, state, and federal elected office. The Women's March is one recent display of Gen Zers' feminist-oriented activism. If politics truly is a virtuous cycle that rewards those who show up, the Women's March proved young women are the bedrock of the contemporary American electorate and the future of political leadership. Gen Zers will take up the mantle of the generations of women before them who fought for equal rights and made it possible for these Gen Zers to go to school, get jobs, and vote. The heroes of this next crisis period may very well be young women.

---

131 Carrie Elizabeth Blazina and Drew DeSilver, "A Record Number of Women Are Serving in the 117th Congress," *Pew Research Center*, January 15, 2021.

132 Lisa Lerer and Sydney Ember, "Kamala Harris Makes History as First Woman and Woman of Color as Vice President," *The New York Times*, January 11, 2021.

133 Ibid

8

THE AOC EFFECT

It's June 26, 2018. New Yorkers are turning out to the polls to vote in the primary election to decide which candidates will represent each party in the midterm Congressional elections come November. There are a few contested races to watch. Joseph Crowley's is not one of them. The ten-term Democratic incumbent for New York's 14th congressional district is deeply ingrained in the fabric of the Democratic establishment and central to the party machine.[134] At the time of the primary, he was serving as Chair of the House Democratic Caucus, and his name was being floated as a nominee for Speaker of the House.[135] Crowley's lock on Queens was so strong that no one had dared to run against him in the Democratic primary since 2004.[136]

This year was different. In an election year that eventually became known as the "Blue Wave" election, there was an appetite for more progressive Democratic candidates.

---

134 James Arkin and Scott Bland, "Top Democrat Crowley Loses in Shocker," *Politico*, June 26, 2018.
135 Ibid.
136 Ibid.

Crowley faced a primary challenge from a young progressive candidate, a twenty-eight-year old woman from the Bronx who had never held elected office and worked as a waitress and bartender at a taqueria in Union Square.[137] Three weeks before the election, Crowley led his opponent by thirty-six points.[138] He had the endorsements of Democratic Party establishment heavyweights like Governor Cuomo and Senator Chuck Schumer.[139] When the final vote tally came in, Crowley had been defeated by fourteen points.[140] His opponent had managed to pull off a fifty one point swing to claim victory in the primary and would go on to win the general election in New York's 14th congressional district.[141] Her name was Alexandria Ocasio-Cortez.

***

Ocasio-Cortez' victory pushed members of the Democratic Party establishment to realize that in the era of modern politics, they can no longer stand on the shoulders of their party and cross their fingers to hope it will be enough to carry them over the finish line. They must make their appeal to both Millennials and Gen Zers, who collectively comprise the largest share of the American electorate. If they can mobilize these voters by talking about the issues that matter to them, they can claim victory. These candidates must also work to

---

137 David Remnick, "Alexandria Ocasio-Cortez's Historic Win and the Future of the Democratic Party," *The New Yorker*, July 16, 2018.

138 Alexandria Ocasio-Cortez, interview by Stephen Colbert, *The Late Show with Stephen Colbert*, June 28, 2018.

139 "Endorsements," Crowley for Congress, accessed July 20, 2020.

140 Alexandria Ocasio-Cortez, interview by Stephen Colbert, *The Late Show with Stephen Colbert*. June 28, 2018.

141 Ibid.

undermine voter suppression efforts that disproportionately bar young people and people of color from going to the polls. The future of the Democratic Party lies in this young, diverse, progressive voter coalition that AOC has become the figurehead for.

Ocasio-Cortez's victory was billed as the greatest upset of the 2018 primary election cycle. She was the bellwether of change in both Congress and the Democratic Party on a national level. Her election, as well as that of the other freshmen women who make up what is informally known as "The Squad," ushered in a more progressive era for the Democratic Party in 2018. This young, progressive freshman caucus terrified conservatives. Ben Shapiro, Editor of the *Daily Wire*, podcast host, and staunch conservative, said AOC is a member "howling at the moon branch of the Democratic Party" that "throws out radical proposals" and then claims "moral clarity lies in making proposals that are completely untenable and never will be paid for."[142] In a segment on his show, Tucker Carlson said, "Alexandria Ocasio-Cortez is a moron and nasty and more self-righteous than any televangelist who ever preached a sermon on cable access. She's not impressive, she's awful."[143] In the same segment, Carlson praised Ocasio-Cortez, saying, "She is one of the very few people who will say the obvious about growing corporate tyranny in this country."[144]

---

142 Ben Shapiro, interview by Martha MacCallum, *The Story with Martha MacCallum*, June 27, 2018.

143 Tucker Carlson, "AOC Has the Cure for Human Extinction," April 1, 2019, on *Tucker Carlson Tonight*, video, 5:30.

144 Ibid.

Even her most steadfast critics can recognize the power of her messaging and the importance of the issues she lends her powerful voice to. Conservatives like Shapiro and Carlson continue to publicly lambast her due to her status as a rising Democratic star and champion of progressive causes. Her platform is antithetical to everything conservatives stand for, which has made her a prime target for ridicule from Republicans. Still, she stands as a beacon of hope for young progressives. Stephanie Fragoulias, a political science student from New Jersey, said of Ocasio-Cortez, "She intimidates traditional politicians by bringing in such radical ideas; however, she is authentically herself. I am inspired by such bravery."

***

Ocasio-Cortez became the youngest woman to ever serve in the United States Congress when she took office at twenty-nine years old.[145] She's a Millennial, but a major part of how she was able to pull off her primary upset was by turning out those first-time Gen Z voters in 2018. Ocasio-Cortez recalls the moment she knew something had changed on election night: "We were about eight minutes until the polls were closing and I was in my home neighborhood in the Bronx… and these two teenage-looking kids came up to me and were like, 'We just voted for you!' And I was like, 'How old are you?' and they're like, 'Nineteen!'"[146] She noted how extraordinary it was that teenagers had voted in a primary election in a midterm year, as they are by no means considered to be

---

145 David Remnick, "Alexandria Ocasio-Cortez's Historic Win and the Future of the Democratic Party," *The New Yorker*, July 16, 2018.

146 Alexandria Ocasio-Cortez, interview by Stephen Colbert, *The Late Show with Stephen Colbert*, June 28, 2018.

among the reliable voters that the pollsters had been surveying. Ocasio-Cortez said of her victory, "We changed who turns out and that changed the whole electorate."[147]

It was a model for youth engagement that the Democratic Party establishment had yet to fully embrace, but one Ocasio-Cortez and other young progressives saw great promise in. She won her 2020 primary race with over 70 percent of the vote.[148]

Her overwhelming 2018 primary victory reflects the strong base of support she has among her constituents. Ocasio-Cortez's background as a Bronx native with strong roots in the neighborhood were apparent in every facet of her campaign. She looks, talks, and acts like her constituents; they see her as not just a politician, but a neighbor. Alex Joshua, a conservative from New Jersey, told me he was "happy to see working people like Alexandria Ocasio-Cortez in Congress, even if [he doesn't] agree with her." She represents average Americans and is a disruption to the status quo of career politicians in Washington who become out of touch with the voters in their home districts.

***

Ocasio-Cortez built her campaign on issues young voters care about like healthcare, education, and income equality. She was rewarded handsomely for her efforts to appeal to and mobilize the youngest voters in her district. Changing

147 Ibid.
148 Clare Foran, "Alexandria Ocasio-Cortez Wins Democratic Primary Against Michelle Caruso-Cabrera, CNN Projects," *CNN*, June 24, 2020.

the narrative—that the reason young people do not turn out is because they do not care—is imperative to getting young people to fully participate in the political process. AOC understood that, and it landed her a seat in Congress while propelling her to national political stardom.

While politicians on both sides of the aisle have villainized Ocasio-Cortez for her progressive platform, they could learn a thing or two from her ability to successfully launch a campaign that turned out historically unlikely primary voters. People like those teenagers she ran into on election night are the future of American politics. The future of the Democratic Party may not hold the promise of all those ambitious Democratic Socialist policies AOC has become known for promoting, but it does include a coalition that is comprised of those young, diverse voters that she most appeals to.

9

THE PROUD
GENERATION

―――

"Although the limitation of marriage to opposite sex couples
may long have seemed natural and just, its inconsistency with
the right to marry is now manifest, it would diminish the
personhood of same-sex couples to deny them this liberty."
With these words, Justice Anthony M. Kennedy delivered the
5–4 opinion in *Obergefell v. Hodges* (2015) that made same-
sex marriage legal in the United States of America.[149] On the
steps of the Supreme Court of the United States, LGBTQ+
activists and allies waited anxiously to hear the opinion of
the Court. They waved rainbow flags and donned the logo
of the Human Rights Campaign on their shirts. They knew
they were bearing witness to a historic moment.

Supreme Court interns made the quarter-mile sprint from
the Court's exit to the press bay at the bottom of the steps
to deliver the opinion to their respective news outlets. The

―――

149 Obergefell v. Hodges, 576 U.S. 644 (2015).

crowd roared as the opinion was announced and exploded with joy into a rendition of the "Star-Spangled Banner." It was a moment many in the crowd had been dreaming of for many, many years.

That night, the White House was lit up in rainbow lights, a symbol of LGBTQ+ pride, in celebration of the historic decision. First Lady Michelle Obama was so elated by the decision that she and her daughter Malia hatched an elaborate plan to sneak out of the White House so they could be amongst those crowds celebrating the decision.[150] Across the country, same-sex couples rushed to courthouses to procure marriage licenses. One of the largest social movements in US history was celebrating a hard-fought victory that was decades in the making. Gen Zers are carrying on the legacy of several generations of LGBTQ+ activists that came before them by becoming politically active at a young age. One day, many of these Gen Zers may take it a step further and run for office.

***

For this chapter, it is essential to look back on the decades of LGBTQ+ activism that laid the groundwork for contemporary activists by transforming public opinion. In the late twentieth century as more LGBTQ+ Americans came out, they were met with social and political backlash. During a riot at the Stonewall Inn in New York City in the 1960s, a movement was born with the purpose of advocating for LGBTQ+ Americans. During the AIDS crisis in the 1980s,

---

150 Alexander Kacala, "Michelle Obama Reveals She Snuck Out of White House to Celebrate Gay Marriage Ruling," NBC News, November 16, 2018.

stigma mounted as medical experts warned of "gay cancer" and blamed the epidemic on what they described as the promiscuous activity of gay men. Members of the LGBTQ+ community were continuously exiled from American society and demonized by the politicians they hoped would support their cause.

Groups like ACT UP (AIDS Coalition to Unleash Power) demanded the Food and Drug Administration provide terminally ill patients with experimental drugs.[151] Their anger and grief were encapsulated in public displays of militant-style activism.[152] In large marches, "members paraded through the streets of New York and Washington, frothing with anger and burning paper effigies of FDA administrators, their argument ricocheted potently through the media and public imagination."[153]

Through ACT UP, LGBTQ+ Americans emerged as a political force. They organized a large-scale protest movement known for its unconventional demonstrations and vocal members. The street activism of ACT UP was designed to disrupt the lives of, and sometimes offend, politicians, bureaucrats, and big pharma executives. Their protests countered homophobic discourse that intended to publicly shame and consequently silence AIDS victims. The politicization of AIDS contributed to increased recognition of LGBTQ+ discrimination and facilitated activism that served as a rebuke of heteronormativity.

---

151 Siddartha Mukherjee, *The Emperor of All Maladies: A Biography of Cancer*, (New York: Scribner, 2011), 319.

152 Ibid.

153 Ibid.

In the late 1990s, the LGBTQ+ community began to gain broader acceptance in social and political circles. LGBTQ+ representation increased in the media with shows like *Will & Grace*, *Ellen*, and *Friends* featuring storylines centered around LGBTQ+ characters.[154] This positive representation cast the LGBTQ+ community in a new light and promoted societal acceptance of the causes championed by LGBTQ+ activists, including the legalization of same-sex marriage. Gen Z babies were born into an American society that was slowly, but steadily, becoming increasingly accepting of the LGBTQ+ community.

LGBTQ+ representation increased in the 2000s as same-sex marriage became legal in states like Massachusetts, Connecticut, and New Jersey. In 2004, the year Massachusetts became the first state to allow same-sex marriage, just 31 percent of Americans were in favor of legalizing same-sex marriage.[155] By 2019, that number had risen to 61 percent.[156] This major shift in public opinion happened during the initial political socialization for Rebuilders, the eldest members of Generation Z.

***

When *Obergefell v. Hodges* was decided in 2015, Gen Zers were in the midst of attempting to form their own beliefs

---

154 Lauren B. McInroy & Shelley L. Craig, "Perspectives of LGBTQ Emerging Adults on the Depiction and Impact of LGBTQ Media Representation," *Journal of Youth Studies* 20, no. 1, (2017), 32-46.

155 Pew Research Center, "Attitudes on Same Sex Marriage," *Pew Research*, May 14, 2019.

156 Ibid.

about LGBTQ+ rights issues. Ryan Wolfe listed *Oberge-fell* as a defining moment in the formation of his political identity because it made him realize "that things were bigger than just me and my small town in Iowa. I realized at that moment how big the world was." Exposure to people of differing sexual orientations and gender identities fighting for their civil rights made Generation Zers sympathetic to LGBTQ+ causes. Allyship between young, straight Americans and their LGBTQ+ counterparts is a key component of Gen Z's collective identity. *Obergefell* helped cement that by creating a shared historical experience centered around LGBTQ+ rights.

Keith Nagy, the National Political Affairs Director for the College Democrats of America, also pointed to *Obergefell* as one of the key events that influenced his political identity. Nagy, who is openly gay, grew up in rural Kansas. For him, the struggle for LGBTQ+ rights is "very personal." He noted his hometown is not far from the Westboro Baptist Church, an organization that is infamous for its homophobia. Yet Nagy is encouraged by the progress the United States has made on LGBTQ+ rights issues. Nagy said the *Obergefell* ruling was a "reminder of exactly how far we've come as a country, but also that there's still a lot of progress to be made in various aspects of civil rights."

In the span of just over a decade, Rebuilders witnessed same-sex marriage go from being illegal in all states to being legal in every state in the union. Travis Legault, who is active in LGBT Democratic politics, said, "I consider myself really fortunate to have been born at the time that I was. The 2010s were so important for LGBT folks."

Growing up in this era of increasing LGBTQ+ acceptance and public awareness of LGBTQ+ rights issues was important for Legault. He recalls the "It Gets Better" campaign, a movement to prevent suicide among LGBTQ+ youth, as a formative event in his lifetime.[157] Legault told me, "There were a lot of youth suicides and some of those kids who were LGBT were about the same age as I was. I was grappling with my sexuality, I hadn't come out yet, and I was just starting to come out to myself." He went on to add, "I distinctly remember President Obama and Joe Biden coming out in favor of marriage equality in 2011 and then making videos for the It Gets Better campaign. It's something I remember really well." For young LGBTQ+ Gen Zers coming to realizations about their sexuality, the developments of the 2010s offered hope that it truly would get better for the entire LGBTQ+ community.

The refusal of many young Americans to be constrained by heteronormative attitudes and the gender binary has exposed Gen Zers to people all along the sexuality and gender spectrums. This has resulted in Generation Z being more accepting of non-heterosexual and non-binary people than any other generation, including Millennials. American Gen Zers are also more likely to identify as queer than any other generation. In a study done by J. Walter Thompson Innovation Group, only 48 percent of Gen Zers identify as exclusively heterosexual.[158] For comparison, 65 percent of millennials aged twenty-one to thirty-four identify as exclusively

157 Brian Stelter, "Campaign Offers Help to Gay Youths," *The New York Times*, October 18, 2010.

158 Graeme Allister, *JWT: Generation Z- Executive Summary*, (New York: J. Walter Thompson Intelligence, May 2019.

heterosexual.[159] Gen Zers are also more likely to know someone who uses gender-neutral pronouns. Only 43 percent of people aged twenty-eight to thirty-four know someone who goes by "they," "them," or "ze," compared to 56 percent of people aged thirteen to twenty.[160] Gen Zers have more interactions with people who prefer gender-neutral pronouns, which has helped to normalize this practice. This correlates to the belief that 81 percent of Gen Zers have: gender does not define a person as much as it used to.[161]

It's not that more young people are queer than in other generations, rather it's that more young people are realizing they do not fit into the strictly heterosexual or cisgender boxes society has attempted to confine them to. It also speaks to a culture that is more accepting of people who come out as queer, transgender, or non-binary. As American society has become more inclusive of queer and non-binary people, teens are discovering there are more accurate terms to describe their sexuality or gender identity. Teens are also becoming comfortable with the idea of not putting a label on their sexual orientation or gender identity at all. That is also in large thanks to the internet, which has allowed people to access information about sexuality and gender identity and join digital communities that facilitate this process of self-discovery. The internet also serves as an educational resource for straight and/or cisgender allies who want to learn more about the LGBTQ+ community.

159 Ibid.
160 Ibid.
161 Kim Parker and Ruth Igielnik, "On the Cusp of Adulthood and Facing an Uncertain Future: What We Know about Gen Z So Far," *Pew Research Center*, May 14, 2020.

***

These beliefs appear radical to those who have continuously exploited changing attitudes about gender and sexuality as partisan social issues, rather than as human and civil rights issues. For the 2020 election, the Trump campaign recycled the 2016 GOP (Grand Old Party) platform, which in part called for the nomination of federal judges who would overturn *Obergefell*.[162]

The truth is, the GOP are startlingly behind on LGBTQ+ issues. This was the case before Trump took office. Reagan infamously did not even utter the word "AIDS" publicly until 1985, four years after the syndrome had been identified.[163] LGBTQ+ Americans are among the staunchest Democratic supporters, especially amongst Gen Zers. A PRRI/MTV Survey found that just 8 percent of young LGBT Americans identify as conservatives; this is in contrast to 25 percent of their straight peers.[164] This bodes poorly for the future of the GOP as young LGBT Americans are more politically active than young, straight people.

On average, LGBT youth participated in 1.6 more political activities than their straight counterparts.[165] Members of the

---

162 Republican National Committee, "Resolution Regarding the Republican Party Platform," published August 24, 2020.

163 Andrew L. Johns ed, *A Companion to Ronald Reagan*, (Chichester, UK: Wiley Blackwell, 2015).

164 Alex Vandermaas-Peeler, Daniel Cox, Molly Fisch-Friedman, Robert P. Jones, "Diversity, Division, Discrimination: The State of Young America," *Public Religion Research Institute*, January 10, 2018.

165 Melissa Deckman, and Mileah Kromer, "Young LGBT Americans Are More Politically Engaged Than the Rest of Generation Z," *The*

"activist class" in Gen Z, the young people most likely to run for elected positions in government, are more likely to identify as LGBTQ+. In a survey of 410 participants aged eighteen to twenty-four enrolled in IGNITE, a nonprofit that teaches women how to run for office, 28 percent of respondents identified as LGBT.[166] None of the LGBT respondents identified as either conservative or Republican. This shows just how steadfast the community is in supporting the Democratic Party. Going forward, it is incumbent on the GOP to reflect on their party's views of core LGBTQ+ rights, including but not limited to, same-sex marriage, workplace discrimination, and transgender people serving in the military.

The 2018 midterm elections marked a watershed moment for LGBTQ+ representation in office. A historic high of 627 openly LGBTQ+ candidates ran for office, according to Victory Fund (a PAC supporting LGBT candidates).[167] In the years to come, that number should only increase as more Millennials enter electoral contests and Gen Zers become eligible to run for office.

The American electorate is becoming increasingly openly queer as Millennials and Gen Zers comprise a larger share of the eligible voting population. Since they are disproportionately likely to be politically active, progressive LGBTQ+ activists will also be disproportionately overrepresented in young voter turnout. This makes them one of the most influential voting blocs among the Millennial and Gen Z cohorts.

Conversation, June 28, 2019.

166 Ibid.

167 Elliot Imse, "The Rainbow Wave May Touch down in State Legislatures," *Victory Fund*, November 5, 2018.

They are fueled by the hope instilled in them by the image of the White House lit up in rainbow colors after the *Obergefell* ruling. It was the first time many of them had truly felt like the government was on their side and that a more just and equitable America for LGBTQ+ people was on the horizon. LGBTQ+ people and their allies are an increasingly powerful political force in America. They utilize effective methods of communication by constantly pushing and often creating new avenues for representation in various forms of media (magazines, podcasts, TV shows, web series, movies, and books).

The youngest members of the LGBTQ+ community already outpace their peers in their activism, amplifying their voices so those in the highest levels of government are inclined to address issues facing their community in order to access their large mobilizing force. As more LGBTQ+ people join the ranks of government and gain a larger share of the American electorate, it is imperative both parties acknowledge their political power and address the concerns being raised by LGBTQ+ Americans.

Right now, these LGBTQ+ activists are looking to the Biden-Harris administration in hopes they will address continued discrimination against the community. Years ago in 2012, then-Vice President Joe Biden became the highest-ranking government official to voice support for the legalization of gay marriage.[168] A few weeks later, he was reported to have told the mother of a transgender woman that fighting

---

168 Emily Wax-Thibodeaux, "Biden's Ambitious LGBT Agenda Poises Him to Be Nation's Most Pro-equality President in History," January 11, 2021.

against transgender discrimination was the "civil rights issue of our time."[169] Biden became the first president to have an openly gay official confirmed by the Senate to serve in his Cabinet in the form of Secretary of Transportation Pete Buttigieg.[170] Many areas remain for the Biden administration to improve on LGBTQ+ public policy, and ample opportunities to engage a young, politically active cohort of LGBTQ+ Americans. In the future, Americans can expect many more LGBTQ+ people to become prominent figures in the national political arena.

---

169 Ibid.

170 "President-Elect Biden Announces Mayor Pete Buttigieg as Nominee for Secretary of Transportation," Biden-Harris Transition, updated December 15, 2020.

10

PETE FOR AMERICA

It is February 3, 2020. The first primary contest of the 2020 elections is underway. The Democratic field is packed with experienced candidates, including Democratic heavyweights like former Vice President Joe Biden (as he was known then), Senator Bernie Sanders, and Senator Elizabeth Warren. As caucus day approaches, one candidate continues to surprise even the most experienced pundits by polling at the top of the field. An openly gay Millennial veteran who can speak seven languages, who is a Harvard graduate and Rhodes Scholar, and whose only political experience is serving as mayor of a small town in Indiana.[171] His name was Pete Buttigieg, and he would go on to win the 2020 Iowa Caucus. His historic victory made him the first openly LGBT candidate to win delegates in a presidential primary contest.[172] Pete Buttigieg is representative of a new class of Millennial leaders who are offering a forward-thinking vision of American politics.

---

171 Anthony Zurcher, "Pete Buttigieg: How a Young, Gay Mayor Became a Democratic Star," *BBC News*, April 9, 2019.

172 Barbara Rodriguez, "Pete Buttigieg Made History in the Iowa Caucuses Whatever the Final Results Show," *Des Moines Register*, February 5, 2020.

This chapter will explore how "Mayor Pete" beat the odds to win the Iowa Caucus. His young age, outsider status, and intellectual background made him an underdog worth rooting for. Buttigieg's Obama-adjacent message of hope promised a more proactive, efficient government; this attracted attention from his fellow Millennials and Generation Z. He offered a new playbook for the Democratic Party that looked unabashedly toward the future to a more progressive, inclusive caucus.

Amongst a field of older candidates with deep ties to the Democratic establishment, Mayor Pete offered a candidacy that was infused with youthful energy while still drawing upon his own strong moral and intellectual foundation. His age made him stand out from the crowd, while his character appealed to the most educated and diverse generations in American history. Buttigieg's message evoked a sense of hope that mirrored that of Obama's 2008 campaign. Nick Roberts, a staunch Buttigieg supporter, remarked, "Obama's 'Yes We Can,' as cliché as it is, is a winning message if we have the right messenger."

Mayor Pete was looking to build a coalition of voters not dissimilar to that of President Obama, focused on Millennials and voters in America's heartland. Obama was a first-term senator when he ran for office. Buttigieg had not held an office higher than that of mayor when he entered the 2020 race.[173] Both offered a truly new perspective on national politics that was rooted in a healthy skepticism of the traditional

---

173 Zurcher, "Pete Buttigieg: How a Young, Gay Mayor Became a Democratic Star."

Washington-centric political establishment. They both displayed profound respect for democratic norms and the political process, a key feature that distinguishes their claims to "outsider status" from Donald Trump's.

Buttigieg's outsider appeal led many to draw comparisons to Donald Trump, but they could not be more different. The key difference between them is not just their basic disagreements on the issues, but their differing visions for America. Donald Trump's slogan "Make America Great Again" intentionally invokes the idea America was once great, and we should return to that state. It is a message that looks backward. Pete Buttigieg, like his fellow Millennials, refuses to look anywhere except forward. That strong moral and intellectual foundation means simultaneously recognizing the failings of government while acknowledging its capacity to be a vehicle for meaningful progress. Millennials and Gen Zers distrust government but want it to take a more active role in solving America's most pressing problems.[174]

**

Buttigieg told *The Daily Show*'s Trevor Noah why he thinks he appeals to voters: "I'm from a new generation, which I think raised some eyebrows early on, but I think it's one of the reasons why it makes sense to do this."[175] Buttigieg's campaign was the first time Americans saw what a Millennial

174 John Della Volpe, "The Role of Young Voters in 2020," interview by Kerri Miller, *MPR News with Kerri Miller*, MPR News, April 27, 2020, audio, 50:02.

175 Pete Buttigieg, interview by Trevor Noah, *The Daily Show with Trevor Noah*. February 6, 2020.

politician was capable of achieving in a national election. He offered hope that the next crop of Democratic leaders would be representative of the Millennial generation. That would mean more progressive politicians, members of the LGBTQ+ community, people of color, women, disabled people, and people of diverse faith backgrounds populating the halls of the Capitol building.

Buttigieg's relatively young age, lack of experience in national politics, and educated background made him relatable to the average Democratic voter. He had lived through the major events of the past three decades as a concerned citizen. He did not just live through the War on Terror—he fought in it.[176] He did not just experience the Great Recession—he spearheaded the economic recovery of South Bend, Indiana in the wake of it.[177] He did not just live through the LGBTQ+ rights movement—he lived as a closeted gay man in America until he came out right before the Supreme Court declared same-sex marriage legal in America.[178] Ryan Wolfe, who also comes from Midwestern roots, pointed out, "His historic campaign marked an important shift in the American electorate's views on social issues…[his success] shows the growth of support for LGBTQ+ [people] within the American electorate over the past decade."

176 Zurcher, "Pete Buttigieg: How a Young, Gay Mayor Became a Democratic Star."

177 Michael J. Hicks, "An Indiana Economist Looks at South Bend's Revival Under Buttigieg," *MarketWatch*, April 19, 2019.

178 Nik DeCosta-Klipa, "Pete Buttigieg Explains Why He Didn't Come Out until Nearly His Second Term as South Bend Mayor," *Boston.com*, April 3, 2019.

Buttigieg's Midwestern-nice style and Obama-adjacent oratory style were refreshing and real and made him seem more moderate than he was. He stuck out like a sore thumb among a field of candidates populated by well-known members of the Democratic Party. Many candidates came into the race with higher name recognition, including Representative Beto O'Rourke, Senator Cory Booker, and then-Senator Kamala Harris. Buttigieg managed to defeat the odds and outlast most of the field, eventually competing with party figureheads like Senators Warren, Klobuchar, and Sanders, as well as Joe Biden in early primary contests.

***

With Warren and Bernie Sanders monopolizing the progressive wing of the party, Buttigieg was forced to move closer to the center. Ryan Wolfe noted that Buttigieg "start[ed] his campaign with support for Senator Bernie Sanders' Medicare-for-All plan and the House-passed Green New Deal but shifted his support to more moderate policies with similar goals." These moves made him fall out of favor with young progressives.

Buttigieg's downfall was ultimately that he had not done enough outreach to Black voters and by virtue of his sole political experience as mayor of South Bend, Indiana, had not demonstrated he could build a national voter coalition of diverse individuals. Wolfe pointed this out as well, telling me, "One criticism I agree with and would not be a complete assessment of him as a candidate is his lack of support within the African American community. You simply cannot win without the support of black voters and those connections and trust need to be built, not expected." In the 2020 South Carolina presidential primary, a state where 57 percent of Democratic voters are Black, Buttigieg received a dismal 2 percent of the Black vote.[179] He dropped out of the race the next day.[180] Nonetheless, Buttigieg represents a new model for Democratic candidates: young, educated, ambitious, open-minded, and unconstrained by societal norms.

Buttigieg gave Millennials and Gen Zers a grasp of the kind of politicians their generations are capable of producing: ambitious candidates with strong moral and intellectual foundations. Coming in first in Iowa put him in the hot seat and made him the default punching bag in the February Democratic debate. When he stood on the debate stage, he was forced to play defense while candidates attacked his status as a newcomer. Buttigieg defended himself, "If we want to beat this president, we've got to be ready to move on from the playbook that we have relied on in the past. We have to unite this country around a new and better vision."[181] This quote sums up much of why Buttigieg is so appealing: He is ushering in a new era of political leadership and offering a reimagined vision of governance. Nick Roberts, a fellow Hoosier and ardent Buttigieg supporter, said of him, "I think his youth and fresh face on the national scene made him a popular choice for many to symbolize the change in guard."

***

179 Elena Schneider, "Buttigieg Drops Out of Presidential Race," *Politico*, March 1, 2021

180 Ibid.

181 *ABC Democratic Debate*, moderated by George Stephanopoulos, David Muir, and Linsey Davis, aired February 7, 2020, on ABC.

While Pete Buttigieg is not a Gen Zer, his campaign represented the sentiments of the generation as far as being fed up with gridlock in government, the old norms of the political elite class, and the lack of representation for young Americans in the federal government. His steadfast commitment to modernizing American governance and bringing young voters into the political process is the genesis of his political stardom. He also offered a glimpse into the potential for LGBTQ+ individuals to become rising stars in national politics. Buttigieg is now the first openly gay person confirmed by the Senate to lead a Cabinet department. The sub-header to the official announcement of Buttigieg's nomination by then President-Elect Joe Biden read: "Buttigieg is a barrier-breaking and transformational public servant who embodies a new generation of American leadership."[182]

182 "President-Elect Biden Announces Mayor Pete Buttigieg as Nominee for Secretary of Transportation," Biden-Harris Transition, December 15, 2020.

PART IV

ORIGINZ

11

VOTING HABITS

———

America's youth are increasingly progressive and are setting records for voter turnout. This chapter will explore how the congressional gridlock of the 2010s and the election of Donald Trump in 2016 have mobilized young voters in record numbers. It will argue that a desire for a more active and larger government, as well as the personal effects of Trump's presidency on American youth, account for the significant role young people played in 2018's "Blue Wave" election.

Despite this, young voters in Generation Z and the Millennial Generation are still less likely to vote than older generations. Research from Professor Mindy Romero will counteract the narrative that young voters have lower turnout because they are apathetic and raise the idea that young people are subjected to voter suppression efforts. The ability of teenagers and twenty-somethings to vote at high rates in 2018 provides hope young people will continue to overcome the obstacles that prevent them from voting. The statistical bump in youth voter turnout will have to be sustained through reinvestment in civics education and mass mobilization efforts focused on the youngest portion of the American electorate.

The political landscape of the 2010s has inevitably had a profound effect on Generation Z and will continue to influence their perception of politics and the role of government. This is due to the fact that in the early teenage years, political views and belief systems are not yet fully formed. The political environment that an individual interacts with when they are approximately fifteen to twenty years old shapes their long-term political beliefs and view of government. Teenagers I interviewed lamented the gridlock that has plagued Congress throughout the past decade and caused a breakdown in government efficiency. This has caused a majority of Gen Zers to believe government should be more involved in actively solving problems in America.[183] They reject small-government ideals and seek leaders who will utilize all the resources at their disposal to solve systemic issues.

THE 2016 ELECTION

Let's take a trip back in time to 2016. Hillary Clinton and Donald Trump are facing off in what many pundits called the most important election of our lifetime. This election would come to mark a pivotal moment in the political socialization of Generation Z. 2016 was the first presidential election that Gen Zers would be eligible to vote in, yet many of them watched the campaigns unfold in horror. Even those who could not vote were captivated by the campaigns of Hillary Clinton and Donald Trump, with many of the Gen Zers I interviewed naming the 2016 election as a pivotal moment in the formation of their political identity. Both Clinton and

---

183 Nikki Graf, Ruth Igielnik, and Kim Parker, "Generation Z Looks a Lot like Millennials on Key Social and Political Issues," *Pew Research Center*, January 17, 2019.

Trump had net negative unfavorable ratings and were disliked by Americans spanning the entirety of the political spectrum.[184]

The unfavorability of both candidates was indicative of intraparty ideological rifts. Democrats chose an establishment candidate who was still committed to delivering some progressive changes in Clinton as opposed to a radical reformer in Bernie Sanders. In a large field of established politicians, Republicans chose a celebrity businessman with a larger-than-life persona whose main goal was to turn Washington on its head. The candidates in the general election could not have been more diametrically opposed or more burdened by personal baggage. Donald Trump ultimately won independents over in a battle best characterized as choosing the lesser of two evils. For some Gen Zers, the 2016 election disillusioned both parties, making them uncomfortable identifying with either side of the aisle.

THE POLITICAL SPECTRUM

In this day and age of hyper-polarized politics, voters may be forgiven for viewing America as a house divided against itself. This image is amplified by pundits on talk shows who engage in shouting matches while disagreeing about basic facts. This has been the model for much of political cable news coverage since the Crossfire era. Taking a step back to look at the big picture of the United States, one will see individuals of all political identities constitute the American

---

184 Sarah Edwards, "Talking Elections," October 19, 2018, in *Talk Policy To Me*, podcast, 27:54.

electorate. Zooming in, one will see no community is entirely red or blue. A lot of America is politically colored in some shade of purple. The past decade of American politics has been chronicled as a battle of which candidates can best toe the party line on the federal level. This completely neglects the vast swaths of land outside of Washington where voters are rejecting party labels.

The phenomenon of the independent and third-party voter is alive and well in America. In local and state-level elections, voters increasingly choose to evaluate a candidate on their character and record rather than simply voting down-ballot for their party preference. I spoke to Ryan Moore, a Libertarian from North Carolina, who routinely votes for Democrats in statewide races and voted for Joe Biden in the November 2020 general election. I also spoke to Ethan Suquet, a Republican from Florida, who told me he planned to vote for Joe Biden in November 2020. I even spoke to Nabila, a self-proclaimed Communist who usually votes for Democratic candidates but believes in the creation of a "classless, stateless society." These are not the only Gen Zers who harbor unconventional political beliefs or occasionally vote across party lines. In a survey conducted by *Business Insider*, more than half of the 1,800 respondents between the ages of thirteen to twenty-one said they did not identify as liberal or conservative.[185] The two-party system as Americans know it is fundamentally changing.

---

185 Kate Taylor, "Gen Z Is More Conservative Than Many Realize—but the Instagram-Fluent Generation Will Revolutionize the Right," *Business Insider*, 2019.

This all speaks to the base of American politics as more moderate than people are led to believe by the national discourse. When Alexis De Tocqueville analyzed the uniquely American brand of democracy (circa the 1830s) in his work *Democracy in America*, he described the circle of thought that dictates which opinions are socially acceptable in the United States. He found these opinions to be moderate in nature as far as they prescribed to the structure of America as a democratic federal republic.[186] Those with opinions outside of the circle of thought are socially exiled.[187]

The modern, wonky explanation of this is the Overton Window, a model of political possibility that shifts based on what political ideas and policies are deemed socially acceptable.[188] An example of this is the evolution of healthcare policy, where in recent years Medicare For All has become a feasible healthcare policy proposal that is openly debated. Americans may fundamentally disagree on radical policy proposals because they are at the fringe of socially acceptable political opinions. Politicians find success moving to the center where popular proposals lie. Joe Biden, who is often hailed as a moderate Democrat, actually ran on the most progressive policy platform ever. It is in the center of the political spectrum that policies like universal background checks for gun purchases fall, a policy proposal that was popular among my interviewees from across the political spectrum.

---

186 Alexis De Tocqueville, *Democracy in America* (Chicago, IL: University of Chicago Press, 2000).

187 Ibid.

188 Mackinac Center for Public Policy, "The Overton Window," published 2019.

From my research, it is evident Americans do not disagree on policy issues as much as they think they do. It is their elected officials who disagree and generate national debates that falsely deepen political, social, and ethnic cleavages in America. This phenomenon of polarization has been exacerbated by years of gridlock. The politicians in Washington appear to be much more polarized than the American electorate is. This is why young voters are rejecting political affiliations and labels. As Matt Post, a field strategist for March For Our Lives said in a radio interview, young voters "are not jaded enough to simply accept the status quo of our politics."[189] Young people are actively shifting the Overton Window and looking for candidates that hold popular policy positions, regardless of their party. If Gen Z becomes more active in politics, policy proposals like the Green New Deal and assault weapons bans will become less radical and more mainstream.

THE TRUMP EFFECT

The election of Donald Trump, an event that had long been deemed impossible by even the most experienced political pollsters and pundits, was a reality. The media had discounted his candidacy from its onset, unable to fathom how a businessman and reality TV star could ascend to America's highest political office. His victory in November of 2016 dumbfounded the political establishment. It was also a hard pill to swallow for Gen Z. According to my interviews with young conservatives, even many Gen Zers who supported

---

189 Matt Post, "What Do Young Voters Want?," interview by James Morrison and Amanda Williams, *Across America*, 1A, February 6, 2019, audio, 29:50.

Trump in 2016 have been disillusioned and strayed from their MAGA ways as they've grown older.

Donald Trump has been the single greatest mobilizing factor for youth turnout in possibly the entire history of American politics. He is wildly unpopular with young voters. I often hear young people musing about what they will tell their children and grandchildren about living during the tumultuous Trump-era. There is something uniquely terrifying about Donald Trump to young voters who have been distrustful of government since they first began watching the news. If years of gridlock, polarization, and corruption undermined their trust in government, Donald Trump was the one who finally destroyed it.

Young progressives and conservatives alike see him as a personal threat. By a margin of 2:1, young voters across the United States aged eighteen to twenty-nine told Harvard's Polling Institute that Donald Trump had caused more harm than good in their personal lives.[190] This is an extremely important motivating factor. A major reason why young people have been reluctant to turn out to the polls is because they do not see themselves or the issues they care about being represented in politics. With Donald Trump, they identify him as someone who is not just ignoring the concerns of young voters but is systematically promulgating negative changes in America.

---

190 John Della Volpe, "The Role of Young Voters in 2020," interview by Kerri Miller, *MPR News with Kerri Miller,* MPR News, April 27, 2020, audio, 50:02.

Young voters were instrumental in the 2018 midterms which has since been referred to as "The Blue Wave" election that served as a major rebuke of Trumpian politics. The general sentiment of young voters is that they are apathetic. The year 2018 proved Gen Zers do not fit that stereotype. Gen Zers turned out in record numbers as many of them (including myself) cast a ballot for the very first time. Midterm turnout is notoriously low, especially among young voters, shockingly, that electoral cohort saw a 79 percent increase in turnout from 2014 to 2018.[191] In 2014, just 20 percent of eligible voters aged eighteen to twenty-nine voted in the midterm election.[192] That increased to 36 percent in 2018, the single greatest percentage point increase in turnout for any age group.[193]

The 2018 midterm election had the highest overall turnout in four decades, while 2014 had the lowest.[194] In some states, early voting numbers exceeded the total 2014 turnout for young voters.[195] Two-thirds of voters aged eighteen to twenty-nine backed Democratic candidates compared to just 32 percent who voted for Republicans, the largest partisan gap in the past twenty-five years.[196] As more Gen Zers become eligible to vote, youth voter turnout is increasing. In 2020,

---

191 Jordan Misra, "Voter Turnout Rates among All Voting Age and Major Racial and Ethnic Groups Were Higher Than in 2014," United States Census Bureau, last modified April 23, 2019.

192 Ibid.

193 Ibid.

194 Ibid.

195 Reid Wilson, "Young and New Voters Surge in Early Voting," *The Hill*, October 31, 2018.

196 Claire Hansen, "Young Voters Turned Out in Historic Numbers, Early Estimates Show," *U.S. News*, November 7, 2018.

Gen Z will surpass the Silent Generation's share of the electorate.[197] There are ample reasons to be hopeful about youth turnout going forward.

Trump was not up for re-election in 2018, but the Blue Wave in the midterm elections served as a personal rebuke of his administration. Midterm elections are seen as referendums on the sitting president because they decide whether his party will gain more or less control in government. The increase in youth voter turnout is reported to have swung at least ten congressional seats to what would ultimately become the Democratic majority in the House.[198]

With Trump on the ballot in 2020, I projected turnout of young voters would increase from 2018 levels. This is due not just to the typical bump in turnout in a presidential election year, but to the Trump effect. Americans should typically expect to see turnout increase by 20 percent from a midterm to a presidential election year, even so, 2020s youth turnout was up from even 2016 levels.[199] According to Tuft University's Center for Information and Research on Civic Learning and Engagement (CIRCLE), 52 to 55 percent of people aged eighteen to twenty-nine, who were eligible to vote, voted in the 2020 presidential election.[200] That number is up 10 to

197 Stef W. Kight, "Deep Dive: 2020's New Voters Will Usher in an Age of Demographic Transformation," *Axios*, December 14, 2019.

198 John Della Volpe, "The Role of Young Voters in 2020," interview by Kerri Miller, *MPR News with Kerri Miller,* MPR News, April 27, 2020, audio, 50:02.

199 Sarah Edwards, "Talking Elections," October 19, 2018, in *Talk Policy To Me,* podcast, 27:54.

200 "Election Week 2020: Young People Increase Turnout, Lead Biden to Victory," Tuft University CIRCLE, published November 25, 2020.

11 percent from 2016.[201] In key states like Michigan, Georgia, Arizona, and Pennsylvania, young people, specifically young people of color, helped Joe Biden claim electoral victory.[202]

Based on interviews I conducted with voters across the political spectrum aged eighteen to twenty-two, I knew young people were ready to vote Trump out of office. Still, in the lead-up to the 2020 elections there were questions about their enthusiasm to turn out to the polls. Bernie Sanders famously blamed his primary losses on lower-than-expected youth turnout. The truth is there is nothing inherently wrong with young people as a demographic and to simply say they are not voting because they do not care is false. The discrepancy between participation in some political behaviors versus voting can be accounted for through youth voter suppression. In 2016, 80 percent of voters aged eighteen to twenty-nine intended to vote but only 43 percent turned out to the polls.[203]

***

It takes experience to navigate voting which places young voters at a severe disadvantage. Their ability to turn out in historically high numbers in 2018 despite voter suppression efforts shows just how significant that election was. Professor Mindy Romero is an expert in youth political behavior. She has found voter suppression and a lack of civic education are significantly affecting youth turnout. In total honesty, voting can be confusing and difficult to navigate for first timers.

---

201 Ibid.
202 Ibid.
203 Ibram X. Kendi, "Stop Blaming Young Voters for Not Turning Out for Sanders," *The Atlantic*, March 17, 2020.

Pre-registration deadlines are massive hurdles to voting and a failure to register as much as two months in advance for an election can preclude someone from voting. Another factor is that young people are highly mobile (think: going to college across the country, internships, and new jobs) and may change addresses and invalidate their voter registration in the process.[204] Confusing voting machines and poorly designed paper ballots can stump voters and derail elections. (I mean, remember hanging chads?)

Voter ID laws are another hurdle to voting that young people must clear which can be complicated if they have not yet received their driver's license. Many young people are working or attending school during the day which may hinder their ability to get to the polls. Precincts can also cause confusion. On my college campus, students are separated into three different voting precincts and must determine where they vote based on what dorm they live in. Civics education was significantly cut in the 1960s right before eighteen-year-olds gained the right to vote.[205] It coincided with a marked decrease in youth voter turnout; that was not a coincidence.[206] Restoring civics education is integral to increasing youth voter turnout.

In Harvard's Institute of Politics Youth Poll, a majority of young voters said they believed they would "see personal

---

204 Mindy Romero, "Why Is Youth Voter Turnout So Low?," filmed May 2016 in Davis, California. TED video, 15:23.

205 Ibid.

206 Ibid.

effects from the outcome of the 2020 election."[207] In other words, young people believe issues they care deeply about were at stake in 2020. According to interviews with young voters, these issues include student loan debt, healthcare, legalization of marijuana, and climate change. What young voters must understand is that politics is a virtuous cycle: vote in larger numbers and politicians will act on the issues that matter to you because they want your vote. The year 2018 showed that, despite voter suppression efforts, young people are making a concerted effort to turn out to vote. They continued that trend in 2020, and politicians are taking notice.

In 2020, Gen Z made up 10 percent of the eligible voting population in the US; as Nick Roberts, a college student from Indiana told me, "There has never been a better time to get people energized." Clearing the hurdles to voting for young people by allowing for same-day registration and online voter registration as well as funding civic education programs could kick-off a decades-long revival of the youth vote.

207 John Della Volpe, "The Role of Young Voters in 2020," interview by Kerri Miller, *MPR News with Kerri Miller,* MPR News, April 27, 2020, audio, 50:02.

12

FEEL THE BERN

———

Across from the steps of the US Capitol building, a small pool of reporters affixed their microphones to the front of a podium. A few passersby and tourists stopped and stared, curious as to who would be holding a press conference on Capitol Hill that attracted so little attention. When the speaker finally emerged from the Capitol building, there was no applause and no roaring crowd to greet him.[208] He sped through the news conference, taking less than ten minutes to make a speech and answer a few questions from the press. The first words out of his mouth that day? "We don't have an endless amount of time. I've got to get back."[209] One would never guess the humble press conference in April 2015 was the start of a political movement. Senator Bernie Sanders had just announced his candidacy for the Democratic Party nomination for president of the United States.

✳✳✳

208 Scott Detrow, "8 Key Moments That Helped Define Bernie Sanders' Presidential Runs," *NPR*, published April 9, 2020.

209 Tamara Keith, "Bernie Sanders 'Stunned' by Large Crowds Showing up for Him," *NPR*, published June 15, 2015.

Senator Bernie Sanders, an Independent from Vermont who caucuses with Democrats, was quickly brushed aside by the media after he announced his candidacy for president of the United States. After all, they figured no one could touch Hillary Clinton, former Secretary of State, Senator from New York, and First Lady of the United States. Clinton was practically Democratic Party royalty and Sanders was a self-proclaimed Democratic Socialist with a small, cult-like following among young people and self-described hippies. Political analysts and pollsters argued Clinton all but had the nomination locked up as long as Vice President Joe Biden and Senator Elizabeth Warren stayed out of the race. Then, the summer of 2015 happened.

Bernie was drawing crowds in the tens of thousands and enjoying massive amounts of support, especially from young Americans, during the summertime.[210] His momentum carried through the end of summer and the fall of 2015, propelling him into a tense primary with Secretary Clinton. The narrative of the 2016 presidential campaign was rapidly shifting as Bernie's grassroots campaign blossomed across the country. At the start of the primary season in early 2016, he almost tied Clinton in the Iowa caucus and beat her by 22 percentage points in New Hampshire. The Clinton campaign realized he was a more serious threat than they had previously considered.[211] In Iowa, some Democratic caucus-goers resorted to coin flips to decide who would win their precinct.[212] Clinton's margin of victory in Iowa was razor-thin.

---

210 Detrow, "8 Key Moments."

211 Ibid.

212 Russell Berman, "Was the Iowa Caucus Decided by Coin Flips?," *The Atlantic*, February 2, 2016.

It was not the triumphant start her campaign had been hoping for.

Strong showings in early contests and grassroots support were not enough to propel Sanders to the nomination. Clinton continued to rack up delegates through the rest of the primary contests in the spring of 2016, gaining an insurmountable delegate lead over Sanders heading into the summer.[213] This lead was accelerated by superdelegates, Democratic Party leaders and elected officials who vote at the Democratic National Convention.[214] Clinton's deep roots in the Democratic Party and her powerful allies in the party establishment gave her the upper hand among superdelegates. Against advice from the Democratic Party, news outlets continued to combine unpledged (a.k.a. superdelegates) and pledged delegates in the delegate counts for candidates. This exaggerated Clinton's primary performance and her delegate lead.

*＊＊

When Clinton became the presumptive nominee, it was a hard pill for Bernie's ardent Gen Z supporters to swallow. Many steadfast Sanders supporters blamed it on what they perceived as the corrupt nominating process of the Democratic Party. I believe the defeat of Sanders, who had vast support among Millennials and first-time Gen Z voters, was a major factor in the low youth turnout for the 2016

213 Gregor Aisch, Josh Katz, Josh Keller, and Alicia Parlapiano, "Clinton's Growing Delegate Lead Is Nearly Unbeatable," *The New York Times*, March 16, 2016.
214 Ibid.

election. Sanders' candidacy was a watershed moment in the formation of Gen Zers' political identities. No matter what their political affiliation is, Conservative, Libertarian, Independent, Liberal, Socialist, or Moderate, interviewees inevitably brought up Bernie Sanders' name in our discussion about their political identity. This was not just because he has become a household name due to his 2016 and 2020 campaigns for president, but because he played a key role in Gen Zers' respective political evolutions. Alex Joshua, a conservative, said of Sanders, "I don't agree with him on virtually anything, but he didn't discount anyone. He focused on young voters and created a movement. He brought more people into the political process and I give him, and really anyone who accomplishes that, credit for doing that."

Sanders talked at length about issues that mattered to teenagers and young adults: student loan debt, healthcare, income inequality, climate change, and racial justice. Ethan Suquet, a conservative from Florida who is part of the policy team at Gen Z GOP, told me he first got interested in politics because of Bernie Sanders' candidacy in 2016. As he did more research, he found he did not agree with Sanders on many issues and realized he was more Libertarian; however, he eventually came to identify as a conservative Republican.

Nick Roberts, vice president of Indiana College Democrats, first became aware of Bernie Sanders through a high school teacher who provided the class with background information on all of the 2016 presidential candidates. Roberts had his interest piqued by the main talking points of Bernie's campaign which, similar to Ethan Suquet, prompted him to further research issues like the legalization of marijuana. The son of a disabled war veteran, Nick Roberts was also fascinated by Sanders' opposition to the Iraq War. Roberts realized he and Sanders had ideological differences, and in 2020 he backed fellow Hoosier, now-Secretary of Transportation Pete Buttigieg. Nonetheless, he was grateful to Sanders for his initial political awakening. Despite their differing political ideologies, the Gen Zers I interviewed credited Sanders for the key role he played in the development of their political identity.

***

The 2016 election was key for Gen Zers since it marked the first time members of the generation could vote in a presidential election, and it served as an agent of their political socialization. Political socialization can best be thought of as a young person's first interactions with the political system. This occurs primarily through family discussions, major news events in their childhood and teenage years, and the elections that occur from the time they are eight to twenty years old. While no members of a generation share identical political views, the significance of Bernie's candidacy amongst interviewees of all political affiliations shows a shared political memory that unites the eldest members of Gen Z.

In the case of Generation Z's eldest members, Rebuilders, the 2016 election stands out as a particularly important event. I'm specifically referring to those Gen Zers born between 1995 and 2002 who were at the peak of their political impressionability during the lead-up to the 2016 election. For those born between 1995 and October 1998, the 2016 election was the first presidential election they were eligible to vote in. For those born between November 1998 and December 2002, it was the first presidential election where they understood the complex policy proposals of the candidates and the political and social context surrounding the election.

The political climate during late adolescence and early adulthood is directly correlated to the development of a political orientation. According to Michael X. Delli Carpini, a political science professor at the University of Pennsylvania, young people are highly impressionable at this age and have loosely defined political belief systems.[215] Key events happening around the ages of fourteen to twenty-two years old create a collective generational perspective. Other events that happened around the time of the 2016 election cycle include the *Obergefell v. Hodges* decision, Brexit, the Pulse shooting, the Charleston Church shooting, the beginning of the Flint water crisis, and the nomination of Merrick Garland to the Supreme Court.

All of these events were extremely impactful in the broader scope of Gen Z's collective political perspective since they occurred in those formative teenage years where political beliefs are constructed. These events cemented gun violence and government inefficiency as two major issues that the United States had to contend with. These beliefs, shaped by major news events in the teenage years of Rebuilders, will remain in Gen Z's collective political consciousness for the

---

215 Michael X. Delli Carpini, "Gen.com: Youth, Civic Engagement, and the New Information Environment," *Political Communication* 17, no. 4 (2000), pages 341-349.

remainder of their lifetime. Bernie Sanders' campaign is one of those core political memories.

***

Bernie's importance to Gen Z comes as a result of his political rise coming at the right time. In a way, his popularity among Gen Zers mirrors Obama's popularity among young Millennials. Both Obama and Sanders garnered massive bases of teenagers and people in their early twenties who were in the process of forming their political beliefs. Both were candidates who spoke at length about issues that mattered most to the youngest voters in the American electorate and delivered them with a message of hope and change.

Bernie Sanders' campaign was a political awakening for Generation Z. Sanders' grassroots movement and ability to mobilize voters is respected on both sides of the aisle and will be remembered as a key agent of political socialization for the eldest half of Generation Z. It is not his exact policies that made him a political icon, but rather his ability to speak on issues like student loan debt, accessible healthcare, the legalization of marijuana, criminal justice reform, and other issues that matter to young voters. Other politicians should seek to replicate Sanders' outreach to young Americans and particularly, people of color. Inviting first-time voters and other young people to participate in the political process by addressing their concerns is essential to the continuity of American democracy.

13

YOUNG REPUBLICANS

———

Reading this book so far, one may be remiss to say Gen Z are a bunch of overly ambitious liberals. One would be missing the point entirely. Young voters from both parties are more progressive than their older counterparts. There are young conservatives and moderate Republicans in Generation Z who are more likely to rebuke traditional Republican stances on small government, climate change, and racial justice. The young Republicans I interviewed for this book have major disagreements with Trump, mostly on budget issues, foreign policy decisions, and moral qualms. Many of them no longer affiliate with the party because of Trump and some of them voted for Joe Biden in the 2020 election. Among Gen Z Republicans, only 59 percent approve of the job that Donald Trump has done in office.[216]

Demographic changes are rapidly occurring as the Millennial generation and Generation Z make up more significant shares of the American electorate with each new cycle.

---

216 Kim Parker, Nikki Graf, and Ruth Igielnik, "Generation Z Looks a Lot like Millennials on Key Social and Political Issues," *Pew Research Center*, January 17, 2019.

Republicans are also facing a critical juncture as they head into the 2020s: Will the party establishment embrace the label of the "party of Trump" or the more moderate views of the party's youngest members? It is a decision that will make or break the GOP's grip on power throughout the next decade.

"Tell them we're not radicals," one young conservative told me when I asked him what he wished older generations understood about Gen Z. These young conservatives are small-government Republicans who are hawkish on foreign policy and more liberal-leaning on social issues. They sport Reagan-Bush sweatshirts. They listen to Ben Shapiro's podcast and read Jonah Goldberg's G-File religiously. They are Bush and Romney fans who view morality, decency, and what they describe as "traditional American values" as the core of Republican politics. Trump's history of alleged affairs, explicit comments, and shady business dealings differ greatly from the buttoned-up, strait-laced personas of the party's past.

***

The most die-hard young Republicans maintain their left-leaning peers in both Gen Z and the Millennial Generation will become more conservative over time. I do not know how true that prediction will turn out to be. In Harvard's youth poll in 2000, voters in older age groups were 2 percent more likely to be Democrats than Millennials.[217] In the 2018

217 John Della Volpe, "The Role of Young Voters in 2020," interview by Kerri Miller, *MPR News with Kerri Miller,* MPR News, April 27, 2020, audio, 50:02.

Harvard youth poll, Millennials were 36 percent more likely to identify as Democrats than older age groups.[218] This thirty-eight-point swing over the course of fourteen years now makes Millennials the most progressive voting cohort in the American electorate (as of 2020).

According to John Della Volpe, the director of the semi-annual Harvard Youth Poll, growing up in post-9/11 America during the Iraq War, entering the job market after the great recession, and being the first generation in American history to be worse off than their parents all made Millennials into the progressive generation they are today.[219] They were also politically socialized during the Obama and Trump eras, a time of extreme political polarization that deepened the divides between both major parties. It remains to be seen how the parties will evolve over the next two to three decades and whether a potential moderation of both parties could lead to a realignment among Generation Z and Millennial voters.

That being said, at this point in time there is no evidence Millennials will become dramatically more conservative over time, and there are no indicators Generation Z will either. Baby Boomers benefitted from long periods of economic growth. Millennials and Generation Z have lived through two recessions so far. Their wealth-accumulation potential is worse than that of their parents' generations, giving them an unfavorable view of the American economy and making them critical of rising income inequality.[220]

---

218 Ibid.
219 Ibid.
220 Ibid.

***

Generation Z may not turn out to be as progressive as Millennials, especially if Trumpian politics meet their demise. That demise could open the door for a new kind of Republican Party: one that embraces the shifting views of the American electorate on issues like income inequality, racial justice, climate change, and healthcare. In some ways, that new conservatism might revert back to traditional GOP values that have been lost in the Trump era, such as allegiance to American allies and a focus on lowering the national debt. The GOP must rise to meet the challenge of adapting to a more diverse electorate or risk consistently losing control the White House in elections throughout the 2020s. In the wake of the historic second impeachment of Donald Trump and the loss of the Republican Senate majority, it seems increasingly likely the Republican Party will be forced to chart a course away from Trumpism to maintain electoral viability.

Many Gen Z Republicans told me they supported or would have supported Trump in 2016 if they were of voting age simply because they favored Republican politicians, a decision many of them now regret. This was especially true with Clinton as the other option on the ballot. Their breaking moments in which they realized they could no longer bite the bullet and vote for Trump in 2020 include everything from his decision to pull out of Syria and abandon the Kurds to the revelation of his affairs with Stormy Daniels and Karen McDougal. For Ethan Suquet, a conservative from Florida, Trump's budget proposal in early 2018, which significantly increased the national deficit, was the straw that broke the camel's back. It made him reflect on why he had previously defended Trump's presidency. Suquet came to the realization that he could not "pinch his nose" and vote for Trump in 2020.

These interviewees view him as a dishonor to the Republican Party as a whole and deplore the way that figures like Senators Ted Cruz and Josh Hawley have bent over backwards to please him. Ryan Moore, now a Libertarian, realized he could no longer identify as a conservative when he saw that the GOP was rallying behind Trump. Moore called Donald Trump "the ugly face of what conservatism...I considered conservatism as moralistic, but I realized that was not true." Moore went on to add, "Trump's popularity showed a side to American conservative thought that did not resonate with me."

Alex Joshua, a conservative from New Jersey, said of the 2016 election that it was "sad to see people bend over to Trump after saying he was unamerican just because they were petrified of Clinton winning." Joshua believes Trump's victory showed the GOP of 2015 to 2020 was "more of a cult of personality rather than a party." Millennial and Gen Z Republicans are starting to move toward the center on many issues including climate change, same-sex and interracial marriage, and racial justice.

The GOP is certainly no longer the party of Reagan and George H.W. Bush, but Donald Trump is *not* emblematic of the voters that constitute the future of the Republican Party. In Harvard's Institute of Politics Spring 2020 Youth Poll, just 32 percent of eighteen- to twenty-nine-year-olds approve of the job Donald Trump is doing as president.[221] Millennial and Gen Z Republicans are reshaping the ideological core of the GOP and will have a profound impact on the party in the coming decade as both voters and candidates. Alex Joshua, a conservative, told me three things he would like to see the Republican Party change its public status on: 1) recognize people of all sexual orientations as humans with equal rights; 2) stop policing the lives of transgender people and start respecting them; 3) focus on women's rights and center the female perspective when discussing the issue of abortion. Joshua pointed to the fact that the GOP recycled its 2016 platform for the 2020 election as a sign of the party establishment remaining out of touch with young voters. As an example, the platform calls for the adoption of a constitutional amendment to ban same-sex marriage.[222]

***

It was clear to Joshua and the other young conservatives I talked to that the GOP is going to become increasingly moderate in the next few years if it wants to maintain its electoral viability. That process started with the defeat of Donald Trump, which Joshua, months before the election, hoped would serve as "a wake-up call to [the GOP] to stop taking their voters for granted." Otherwise, the GOP faces the risk of "becoming politically obsolete in the next ten to twenty years." This is especially true as the United States becomes more ethnically and racially diverse.

---

221 Harvard Kennedy School Institute of Politics, "Harvard Youth Poll," April 23, 2020.
222 Republican National Committee, "Resolution Regarding the Republican Party Platform," published August 24, 2020.

The GOP will have to adjust its views on issues like immigration to win over growing Latino populations in states like Texas, Arizona, and Florida. The Republican Party will also face the challenge of winning over an increasing number of Black voters who care about issues like racial justice, income inequality, and healthcare accessibility, which Democrats have been leading on. Michelle Charles, a Democrat from North Carolina, said "the policies that work for Black people are not the ones the GOP stands for." The GOP needs to reevaluate its policy positions in light of an increasingly diverse electorate.

The GOP will no longer be able to count on older, white voters in rural areas to carry them to electoral victory. If the GOP continues to alienate ethnic minority groups, especially Hispanics and Latinos, they will be defeated in federal election contests for years to come. This means Republicans are going to have to start proposing solutions to issues like police brutality and immigration which are of considerable importance to the Black and Latino populations in the US. They are also going to have to address student loan debt, healthcare reform, gun violence, climate change, and LGBTQ+ rights if they want to appeal to Millennials and Generation Z. This is central to their survival as a party in the decades to come. The question is not if the Republican Party will move closer to the center, but when.

***

In the wake of the attack on the United States Capitol building on January 6, 2021, the ideological divides in the Republican Party are more apparent than ever. The willingness of many Republicans in the House and Senate, most notably Senators Ted Cruz (R-TX) and Josh Hawley (R-MO) and Representatives Louie Gohmert (R-TX), Matt Gaetz (R-FL), and Jim Jordan (R-OH), to give credence to Trump's baseless claims of election fraud is nothing short of an assault on the very foundation of American democracy.[223] Their actions and rhetoric, and that of the president, emboldened supporters who had latched on to these election fraud myths.

The result was a mob of the president's supporters descending on the Capitol in a coordinated attempt "to capture and assassinate elected officials" who they believed were stealing electoral victory from Donald Trump.[224] Just ten Republican representatives voted for Donald Trump's second impeachment, signaling a small minority of Republicans who were willing to rebuke the president's contributions to the violent attack on the Capitol.[225] However, the beginning of the post-Trump era means a reckoning for the Republican Party and an intra-party debate about its future. For now, he retains a chokehold on the party. It is up to voters to determine whether to punish or reward elected officials who remained in lockstep with the president until the very end.

Heading into the 2020s and post-Trump era, the Republican Party faces the daunting task of deciding who to build the party's future around. A one-term, twice-impeached

---

223 Al Jazeera Staff, "Who is Who in the Trump Caucus? Are They the Republican Future?," *Al Jazeera*, January 15, 2021.

224 Brad Heath and Sarah N. Lynch, "U.S. Says Capitol Rioters Meant to 'Capture and Assassinate' Officials - Filing," *Reuters*, January 15, 2021.

225 Weiya Cai, Annie Daniel, Lazaro Gamio and Alicia Parlapiano, "Impeachment Results: How Democrats and Republicans Voted," *The New York Times*, January 13, 2021.

president who left office under the long shadow of the Capitol attack is not the man one wants as the leader of their party. The older, more conservative wing of the party that clung to Trump until the very end has to contend with a younger, more moderate wing who are disenchanted by Trumpism.

Throughout the 2022 and 2024 election cycles, Americans will learn even more about how the GOP approaches demographic changes in the electorate and the remnants of Trumpism within the party. It is important to watch who is considered a rising star within the party to determine whether there is support for a more moderate Republican platform in the near future. I predict it is only a matter of time before the younger, more moderate wing moves the party slightly back toward the center.

14

MADISON CAWTHORN

The year 2020 was a notable election cycle for a plethora of reasons. For the purposes of this novel, it is of utmost importance to point out the 2020 election marked the first time Gen Zers were eligible to run for national office. While some groups like Pew Research Center define Gen Zers as those born between 1997 and 2012, this book uses 1995 as the start year of Generation Z. Article I, Section 2 states, "No Person shall be a Representative who shall not have attained to the Age of twenty five Years, and been seven Years a Citizen of the United States, and who shall not, when elected, be an Inhabitant of that State in which he shall be chosen."[226] This means that in 2020, US citizens born in 1995 were eligible for election to the House of Representatives.

In the 116th United States Congress, the youngest member was thirty-year-old Alexandria Ocasio-Cortez.[227] In the 117th Congress, she was dethroned by twenty-five-year old

---

226 U.S. Constitution, art. I, sec. 2

227 Abigail Hess, "29-Year-Old Alexandria Ocasio-Cortez Makes History as the Youngest Woman Ever Elected to Congress," *CNBC*, November 7, 2018.

Madison Cawthorn, a pro-Trump Republican from North Carolina. While some researchers define him as a Millennial, he is more aptly defined as a Millennial-Gen Z cusper (also known as a "Zillennial," someone born between 1994 and 1998 who shares both Millennial and Gen Z characteristics). Madison Cawthorn represents the quarter of Generation Z with a favorable opinion of Donald Trump but whose views do not exactly align with the establishment Republicans of generations past.[228] Cawthorn was an underdog candidate who proved Generation Z is capable of producing a new wave of young political leaders.

***

To be transparent, I debated whether to include Cawthorn's story in this book. After initially conducting the research for this chapter and writing it, Cawthorn has made more than a few questionable, and in some cases offensive, comments. Ultimately, I decided it was important to include this story in the book. Madison Cawthorn is arguably the most prominent Gen Z Trump supporter. This book seeks to provide a complete overview of Generation Z's political beliefs. It would be revisionist history to exclude Trump supporters from that narrative. The inclusion of this chapter is not a commendation of Cawthorn's words and actions but rather an attempt to tell the story of an elected official who represents the cohort of Gen Zers who did support Donald Trump.

---

228 Kim Parker and Ruth Igielnik, "On the Cusp of Adulthood and Facing an Uncertain Future: What We Know about Gen Z So Far," *Pew Research Center*, published May 14, 2020.

Cawthorn had the cards stacked against him heading into the GOP Primary as he faced opposition from key establishment forces. The seat he was running for was vacated by former Representative Mark Meadows after he took over the post of President Trump's Chief of Staff.[229] Meadows was a prominent figure in Congress where he served as the former chairman of the powerful House Freedom Caucus.[230] In the primary election, Cawthorn faced Lynda Bennett, the vice chair of the Haywood County Republican Party.[231] Bennett closely aligned herself with Trump's administration, earning the President's endorsement of her campaign.[232] She also garnered endorsements from Senator Ted Cruz (R-TX), House Freedom Caucus Chairman Andy Biggs (R-AZ), and prominent conservative groups like the Susan B. Anthony List, Citizens United, American Conservative Union, and the Family Research Council Action PAC.[233] House Freedom Action and the Senate Conservatives Fund both poured hundreds of thousands of dollars into North Carolina's 11th Congressional District on Bennett's behalf.[234] Cawthorn looked to be headed toward a certain defeat on Election Night, despite having spent over $130,000 more than Bennett in his campaign.[235]

---

229 Meagan Flynn, "A 24-Year-Old Novice Beat a Trump-Endorsed Candidate in Primary Race for Mark Meadows' Seat in Congress," *The Washington Post*, June 24, 2020.

230 Jane Coaston, "House Freedom Caucus Founder And Trump Ally Mark Meadows is Retiring from Congress," *Vox*, December 19, 2019.

231 "Biography," Lynda Bennett, published 2020.

232 "Endorsements," Lynda Bennett, published 2020.

233 Ibid.

234 "North Carolina District 11 Race," OpenSecrets, published October 22, 2020.

235 Ibid.

Cawthorn won the primary in what came as a great shock to establishment Republicans.[236] While many considered his defeat a rebuke of Trump-endorsed candidates, that does not capture the full story. Madison Cawthorn has a uniquely compelling personal narrative that is very attractive to Republican voters who are seeking new, young voices in Congress. His life plan was dramatically altered in 2014 when he got into a serious car accident that partially paralyzed him and left him in a wheelchair.[237] After the accident, Cawthorn became a motivational speaker as well as the owner of a successful real estate investment company.[238]

***

While he did not receive President Trump's endorsement in the primary, Cawthorn is unmistakably a pro-Trump Republican.[239] Like other young conservatives, he cares deeply about upholding the Constitution, preserving liberty, and cutting down the national debt.[240] He frequently invokes Reagan when talking about the need to prioritize issues like national security and immigration.[241] He told his supporters on Election Night, "Tonight, the voters of the eleventh district of North Carolina said they're ready for a new generation of leadership in Washington. You turned our message of hope, opportunity, and freedom into a movement." Cawthorn went

236 Flynn, "A 24-Year-Old Novice Beat a Trump-Endorsed Candidate."
237 "About Madison Cawthorn," Madison Cawthorn, accessed October 23, 2020.
238 Ibid.
239 Ibid.
240 "Key Policies," Madison Cawthorn, accessed January 18, 2021.
241 "Issues: American First," Representative Madison Cawthorn, accessed January 18, 2021.

on to add, "While the far left is lighting our cities on fire, we are lifting the light of liberty. Nancy Pelosi and Joe Biden may not be able to control where the Democrats are going, but, together, we can."[242] Cawthorn represent the small cohort of Gen Zers who identify as pro-Trump Republicans. Cawthorn's campaign focused on preventing tax hikes, opposing sanctuary cities, outlawing abortion, and in his own words, combatting "the rise of socialism, especially among my generation."[243]

Cawthorn is a new generation conservative and although he shares many of the same views as establishment Republicans, his young age inclines him to debate issues that matter to young people. He is in favor of removing Confederate statues, albeit through the proper legislative channels and not by protestors.[244] Cawthorn, speaking on the issue of statues honoring Confederate generals, said, "These people seceded from our country. They declared war on the United States. I don't necessarily want to have hero worship for them. I do believe statues romanticize history."[245]

Cawthorn is also less conservative on campaign finance reform than older Republicans. He is in favor of overturning *Citizens United v. FEC* (2010), the Supreme Court case that overruled parts of the Bipartisan Campaign Reform

---

242 Brian Murphy, "24-Year-Old Defeats Candidate Backed by Trump, Meadows in GOP Congressional Primary," *The Charlotte Observer*, June 23, 2020

243 Flynn, "24-Year-Old Novice Beat a Trump-Endorsed Candidate."

244 Elizabeth Crisp, "North Carolina's Madison Cawthorn, 24, Wants to Shake up the GOP: 'It's a Culture War,'" *Newsweek*, July 7, 2020.

245 Tina Nguyen, "Trump Keeps Fighting a Confederate Flag Battle Many Supporters Have Conceded," *Politico*, July 18, 2020.

Act that restricted independent expenditures from corporate entities and labor unions.[246] It's worth noting Citizens United Political Victory Fund endorsed Cawthorn's opponent in the primary.[247]

Cawthorn is still more conservative on most issues than his Gen Z counterparts. On climate change, he said the effect of human activity on the climate is "pretty minimal."[248] Cawthorn views himself as the anti-AOC and explained he "see[s] a significantly higher amount of conservatives in my generation, Gen Z, than I do in the millennial generation."[249] This is not true. Gen Z leans even further left than Millennials and Cawthorn represents the mere 22 percent of Gen Zers who hold a favorable opinion of Trump.[250]

***

Madison Cawthorn jeopardized his position as the new, young face of conservatism with a series of inflammatory comments surrounding the Capitol riot. In December, Cawthorn gave a speech at a conference held by Turning Point USA, a prominent organization for young conservatives.[251] In the speech, he told the crowd, "Call your congressman and

---

246 David Mack, "Most Of Gen Z Leans Left, but Their First Member of Congress Will Probably Be Way to the Right," *BuzzFeed News*, June 27, 2020.

247 "North Carolina District 11 Race."

248 Mack, "Most Of Gen Z Leans Left."

249 Ibid.

250 Parker and Igielnik, "On the Cusp of Adulthood."

251 Kelly McLaughlin, "Republican Rep. Madison Cawthorn Told a Turning Point USA Crowd Last Month to 'Lightly Threaten' Lawmakers If They Didn't Support Claims of Voter Fraud," *Business Insider*, January 12, 2021.

feel free—you can lightly threaten them and say, you know what, if you don't start supporting election integrity, I'm coming after you, Madison Cawthorn is coming after you, everybody's coming after you."[252] On January 6, 2021, the day of the Capitol attack, Cawthorn had a prime speaking spot at the "Stop the Steal" rally where much of the mob convened before marching to the Capitol building.[253] In his speech, Cawthorn told the crowd, "The Democrats, with all the fraud they have done in this election, the Republicans, hiding and not fighting, they are trying to silence your voice. Make no mistake about it, they do not want you to be heard."[254]

Cawthorn's role in perpetuating Trump's false election fraud claims should not be overlooked. After the Capitol attack, he did say of the protestors, "You don't represent me at all. That's not my movement. You're not part of my party one bit if you're taking this kind of extreme action."[255] Even though he denounced the actions after, Cawthorn fell short of taking accountability for the way his rhetoric emboldened Trump supporters to descend on the Capitol. Cawthorn and other Trump supporters in Congress may maintain their MAGA mindset for a period of time, however, it remains to be seen whether Cawthorn is truly the face of the future of the Republican Party. His status in the national political arena will be part of the debate over the Republican Party's trajectory. The 2022 and 2024 election cycles will provide insight

---

252 Ibid.

253 Ibid.

254 Ibid.

255 Olivia Nuzzi, "What Madison Cawthorn Saw at the Insurrection," *Intelligencer*, January 16, 2021.

about whether Trump's most loyal allies will be rewarded or punished by their respective electorates.

While Cawthorn may be the first Gen Zer in Congress, he is far more conservative than his generational peers. Looking to the future, it seems more likely that young progressives will begin to mount primary challenges against incumbents and clear the way for a younger, more progressive congressional delegation. His election could encourage other Gen Zers to run for seats in the House, perhaps in the 2022 midterm elections and the next presidential election cycle in 2024. The 2026 midterm elections will mark the first time that Gen Zers are eligible to run for Senate seats as 1995 babies will reach the age of thirty, the constitutional threshold for senators. A new generation of leaders is set to enter the halls of Congress very soon.

15

ON THE GROUND

They tweet about politics; they write about politics; they read about politics; they take to the street to protest; they take to the polls to vote; they sign petitions; they donate to campaigns; they canvass and phone bank for candidates. They're most active online, but that activity on the internet has translated into tangible action. Generation Z is hitting the ground running to support grassroots candidates and slowly transform the American political system. This showcases their incredible penchant for teamwork during the crisis period, as predicted by Strauss and Howe. This chapter will detail how their mobilization efforts are already beginning to bear fruit as they work on political campaigns, take to the streets to protest, and run for office themselves.

POLITICAL ORGANIZING

Nick Roberts lifts his arm and curls his fingers into a fist. Knock, knock. The sound echoes through the Indiana neighborhood as he waits for the homeowner to open the door. Maybe they will not open at all, or maybe they'll open it and slam it in right in his face. Either way, the anticipation is killing him. Most likely, they won't be able to close it once they see Nick's smiling face as he greets their dog and compliments their beautiful front porch. Canvassing: simultaneously the most important and least appreciated aspect of political campaigning. As Nick Roberts said, "Campaigns are about making connections so that people are more sympathetic to the candidates." He lives for canvassing.

Roberts has met four presidents: Jimmy Carter, Bill Clinton, Barack Obama, and Joe Biden. He has also met Senators Cory Booker and Elizabeth Warren, Speaker of the House Nancy Pelosi, Secretary Hillary Clinton, and author-turned-presidential-candidate Marianne Williamson. Like a true Hoosier, Roberts has met Secretary of Transportation and former mayor of South Bend, Indiana Pete Buttigieg more times than he can count. He's only twenty years old.

After getting interested in politics during the campaigns leading up to the 2016 election, sixteen-year-old Roberts felt defeated as he watched Donald Trump take office. He was not the most ardent supporter of Hillary Clinton, something he regrets in hindsight, but he was dismayed that she had lost. Her loss shook him to his very core and made him question what he knew about his fellow countrymen. How had Donald Trump beat Hillary Clinton? He was at a loss for an answer. His liberal-leaning grandmother encouraged him to get involved in local politics. Roberts sprang into action. He emailed the Marion County Democratic organization and got an internship. Roberts' interest in the 2016 election led to his subsequent foray into local, state, and national political organizing.

The election of Donald Trump ignited a fire in him that had laid dormant since his birth: the heroic disposition that characterizes the Rebuilding Generation. Roberts did not know it yet but, like many of his generational peers, the 2016 election had acted as a primary agent of his political socialization and the catalyst for his political awakening. Forged in the fire of a monumental presidential election at the peak of his political impressionability, his heroic instincts were activating. It was time to get to work.

Since the 2016 election, he has built an impressive political resume. Roberts took a gap semester after graduating high school so he could serve as deputy campaign manager for Poonam Gill's Indiana State Representative Race. He's the president of the College Democrats chapter at IUPUI and the vice president of College Democrats of Indiana. Roberts' name first appeared on local ballots when he ran for State Delegate in his home district. He won the uncontested race. I have a feeling that will not be the last time voters see his name on the ballot.

Even in the midst of the coronavirus pandemic, Nick Roberts donned a mask and hit the streets to work on an Indiana State Senate campaign. His commitment to political organizing, even on the local level, is unwavering. By the way he talks about complex policy issues like climate change and public transit, one would think he was a seasoned DC policy wonk. Roberts talks fast but with rhythm, spitting out information retained from academic papers as if it is his own stream of consciousness. He interjects personal anecdotes and opinions with ease. His high level of political interest and participation lead me to classify him as a member of the Rebuilding

Generation's activist class—that is, those young people most likely to run for office someday.

***

In the fall of 2018, Krissie Palomo began attending college in Tarrant County, Texas and discovered a passion she never knew she had. Around campus and the surrounding area of Fort Worth, Texas, Palomo began to notice a growing number of cars adorned with the same black and white bumper sticker, the bold letters spelling out a name she was becoming increasingly familiar with: BETO. Palomo was eligible to vote in the Senate primary that year but had not been paying close attention to the race and did not vote.

In September of that year, a few friends informed her that then-Representative and Senate candidate Beto O'Rourke was coming to their campus to speak. Immediately, she was hooked. "I will always like hold Beto near and dear to my heart because I remember seeing him and just thinking, wow, I feel so much hope," Palomo told me. She knew she had to get involved in the race, so she volunteered with O'Rourke's campaign. Although he narrowly lost, she had caught the political organizing bug. O'Rourke's campaign had demonstrated to Palomo that Texas was not a strictly red state. Growing up in Tarrant, a red county, she is struck by the evolution that she has witnessed over the past few years. She explained, "After 2018, [the county] was kind of purple and then again in 2020, this past year, we flipped it for Biden. I remember thinking, wow, this is insane. It all started in 2018."

Palomo did not stop with Beto's Senate campaign. She has gone on to work on several other campaigns from mayoral races to presidential elections. In 2019, she reached out to her State House District coordinator in Tarrant County to find out how she could get involved in county politics. Krissie Palomo told the coordinator she wanted to get involved because Beto's campaign made her finally realize she was not alone in her political beliefs. The coordinator told her, "We've been here for so long. We've been waiting for somebody like you to come along." The next day, the coordinator invited Palomo to a Kamala Harris fundraiser (when she was still running for president) in nearby Grapevine, Texas to meet her.

At the event, Krissie was introduced to other Tarrant County Democratic organizers, all of whom marveled at the idea of a young woman getting involved in political organizing. She recalls them saying, "What are you doing here? The youngest people that we have in our meetings are usually people's children that they can't find babysitters for." From there, Palomo got involved in local and county politics, eventually volunteering for Deborah Peoples' campaign when she ran for Mayor of Fort Worth, Texas in late winter and the spring of 2019. Around that time, Beto O'Rourke announced he was running for president and Palomo jumped at the opportunity to volunteer on his campaign. When it hit summertime, Palomo decided she wanted to get involved in a race directly impacting her community.

Working on Candace Valenzuela's campaign, Krissie Palomo saw herself represented in the candidate she was working for. Palomo also found a purpose in political organizing.

Valenzuela, a young woman of color, was running in the Democratic primary for the congressional seat in Palomo's home district. Valenzuela's story resonated with Palomo, who is a young Latina. After watching one of her ads, Palomo decided, "I want to be really close to the campaign. This is how I'm going to dive in. I remember making that my mission." She attended a local meet and greet with Valenzuela, where she "hunted down" her field director and asked if they needed an intern. The answer was a resounding *yes*.

The next day, Palomo had quit her seasonal job as a Christmas elf in the local mall and drove to Valenzuela's house to get started. She hit the ground running: "I remember showing up and then, from the first day, her team was showing me the ropes of everything. *Everything*. From call time fundraising to cutting turf in VAN, which is an organizing tool that most campaigns use." Palomo is evidently grateful for her experience on Valenzuela's campaign: "Every time I remember that I get emotional because they really took a chance on me. I could have possibly never pursued electoral politics past that, but they said, 'Nope, we see promise in her.'"

As the future leaders of our democracy, it is incumbent on politicians and their staffs to ensure young people learn the ropes of organizing sooner rather than later. Obtaining that crucial, hands-on experience was the key in cementing Palomo's passion for organizing. Her experience also shows how minority representation in electoral politics is essential to bringing young people of color into the political process.

Even in the throes of a pandemic, Krissie Palomo was more committed than ever to political organizing. After finishing her time on Candace Valenzuela's campaign, she moved to Austin for college and found a job with the Travis County Democratic Party. When she realized they were underutilizing her skills, Palomo asserted her worth and moved on to a job as a digital organizing assistant with the Texas Democratic Party in the lead-up to the 2020 general election. In her first digital organizing role, Palomo learned even more valuable skills that built on the foundational knowledge she acquired as an intern on Valenzuela's campaign.

After the November election, Palomo turned her sights on a school board runoff election in Austin. While working on that campaign, her boss at the Texas Democratic Party reached out about an opportunity for her to join Jon Ossoff's Senate runoff campaign as a digital organizer. Krissie explained her decision to join another campaign: "With that opportunity, I was sold because, at this point in my life, I will jump at anything more I can do to learn something new. At that point, I was between finals, the school board runoff, and Ossoff's campaign, and I wound up doing all three." She found herself juggling multiple responsibilities: "On election day, I was doing both Ossoff's campaign and calling the last bit of voters to get out and vote before I ran to the polling location to do vote chasing."

For Jon Ossoff, she got to answer questions from voters in Georgia through the campaign email, do constituency services, and even answer Ossoff's Instagram DMs. Even though it was a chaotic and busy time, Palomo said, "I would do that again in a heartbeat. I really loved organizing for Ossoff. That team was amazing. Being able to say that I was a part of their digital team, which has gotten high praise from a lot of people, was great."

Roberts and Palomo represent this activist class: a cohort of teenagers and young adults with political ambitions who are extraordinarily involved in the political process. They started their activism on social media sites like Twitter where they were first exposed to political discussions outside of their local community. Now, many of them are gaining influence in their hometowns and trying to sway the opinion of local and statewide electorates. They see a broken political system, and now they are shouldering the massive burden of attempting to correct it. There is a sentiment among Gen Zers that their generation has the last chance at stopping the effects of climate change, systemic racism, and income inequality before they lead to the complete erosion of our democracy.

PROTESTS

In photos taken at protests around the country, one thing stands out. The majority of the people carrying handcrafted signs with calls for change are extremely young. I began to wonder, why are young people so motivated to attend protests? I soon realized my peers are extraordinarily interested in activisM causes because the causes are personal. From the March to Our Lives to the Women's March and Black Lives Matters protest, Gen Z's activism is based on their individual identities. They also provide a window into what issues this generation is most passionate about.

Protests have become integral to the social and political socialization of Generation Z. Mass mobilization of youth has not been seen on this level since the protests against the Vietnam War in the 1960s and 1970s.[256] In a way, it has become trendy to protest. Gen Zers post aesthetically pleasing infographics to their Instagram stories to spread information about the Black Lives Matter movement, LGBTQ+ rights, climate change, and other issues that matter to them. They're not just posting on their feeds; they're also taking to the streets. Seventy-seven percent of Americans aged thirteen to twenty-five reported that they attended a protest in support of equality for Black Americans.[257] Many older American generations see teen activism as a fad, a result of teen angst-fueled rebellion. This is an overused trope and misrepresents why so many teens are turning out to protests in such large numbers. It speaks to a broader pattern of misunderstanding that has made the relationships between Gen Z and the older American generations so tense.

Gen Z has often been misunderstood by older generations as shallow, tech-obsessed, isolated, lazy, and unnecessarily stressed out.[258] These harmful misconceptions make it difficult for today's youth to raise genuine concerns without them being dismissed on account of their age. Young activists have to fight harder than ever to be taken seriously, even though they are leading the charge on issues of grave importance

---

256 Ronald Brownstein, "The Rage Unifying Boomers and Gen Z," *The Atlantic*, June 18, 2020.

257 Dominic-Madori Davis, "The Action Generation: How Gen Z Really Feels about Race, Equality, and Its Role in the Historic George Floyd Protests, Based on a Survey of 39,000 Young Americans," *Business Insider*, June 10, 2020.

258 David Brooks, "The Age of Coddling Is over," *The New York Times*, April 16, 2020.

like climate change, gun violence, and racial justice. These issues are deeply personal.

Gen Z is inheriting a world that has been ravaged by global warming, high levels of income inequality, and unprecedented political polarization. Through the act of protesting, Gen Zers are actively attempting to draw attention to the changes that need to be made in political, social, and cultural institutions. "We see no other option than to push these changes forward," Ryan Wolfe of Iowa said. "Really the anthem of our generation is: We can't be passive. We have to actually work for change."

Gen Zers believe there is an absence of leadership in government on the issues that matter the most to young people, so young activists have stepped up to fill it. Congress, led by members of the Baby Boomer and Silent Generations, have not taken decisive action on key issues, leading young activists to take up the helm.[259] Nick Roberts of Indiana said, "It's easy [for older generations] to punt on issues that will not affect them, like climate change." It is therefore up to Millennials and Generation Z to adequately address these time-sensitive issues, like climate change, before it is too late. Roberts also noted there is "a devaluation of what is best for our country so [young people] have to pick up all the pieces. Issues like Black Lives Matter and climate change will be pervasive for our generation if we don't act now."

---

259 Andy Kiersz, "Americans over Age 65 Run the Country. Here Are 7 Charts That Show How They Hold More Power Than Everyone Else," *Business Insider*, November 4, 2020.

In an increasingly diverse country, racial inequality presents a major threat to the continuity of American institutions. If large swaths of citizens are not represented in positions of power throughout the public and private sector, it is unlikely governing bodies, corporations, and organizations will be able to work toward the common good of all Americans. As for climate change, it poses the largest existential threat to the American population.[260] Natural disasters will increase in frequency, wiping out entire communities and making some areas of the country uninhabitable.[261] There is no more time to wait.

Young people are eager to take to the streets to address pressing issues because time is not on their side. Waiting to address issues like climate change and gun violence is not feasible and will only serve to exacerbate their effects. Gen Zers cannot sit idly by and hope someone will offer them a seat at the table. Many have realized that they must bring their own chair.

RUNNING FOR OFFICE

"It's not age, it's outlook." This slogan appeared on postcards for the Monroe County Young Democrats of Pennsylvania in the lead-up to the 2019 local elections. On the postcard: an endorsement of Jacob Pride, who was running for town supervisor. Pride also serves as the vice president of the

260 Joshua W. Busby, "Who Cares about the Weather?: Climate Change and U.S. National Security," *Security Studies* 17, no. 3 (September 2008): 468-70.

261 David Wallace-Wells, *The Uninhabitable Earth: Life After Warming* (New York: Crown, 2020), 43-44.

Monroe County Young Democrats of Pennsylvania. He was only a sophomore in college when he was elected to serve on Smithfield Township's board of supervisors. Like Nick Roberts, he's a member of the activist class. Pride had his political awakening earlier than most Gen Zers I talked to and by the 2012 election he knew why he was a Democrat and was angling to get politically involved. At age thirteen, he was volunteering with political campaigns. He planned to go to college in DC but wound up staying in his hometown.

Pride decided to run for town supervisor shortly after starting at East Stroudsburg University. He told me he saw many of his friends leaving for college and vowing to never return, and he wanted to change that. Pride became determined to "give people a reason to stay, to remind them why they want to live here and maybe even start their business here." He wanted to give his generation a voice in the town and address the issues that matter most to them, which often go ignored by local politicians. In his words, politics is "about what gets brought to the table." If young people are not bringing ideas to the table, opportunities to fix the issues they care about are being wasted.

Jacob Pride enjoyed bipartisan support in his campaign for supervisor and found people of all ages and political affiliations liked the idea of introducing a new perspective to the town's management. Of course, there were some detractors, including one person who sent him hate mail and published a letter to the editor which read in part: "[Pride] just does not have the life experience and education for the job." Among his accomplishments after a few months on the job are a complete digital overhaul of the town website, the livestream archival of all town meetings, and new zoning changes allowing for more mixed-use buildings.

There are tens of thousands of other members of Gen Z's activist class out there. While the coronavirus pandemic hindered Nick Roberts from his beloved practice of canvassing in the fall of 2020, young people are still determined to get involved in the political process in any way that they can. As Roberts said, "There is no better time to get people energized than now." Soon, that energy will prompt more and more of them to follow in Jacob Pride's footsteps and run for office.

16

MALALA

———

October 9, 2012. After a busy day of exams, a group of Pakistani schoolgirls boarded onto a small bus.[262] Many of the girls used to travel home from school on foot, until their parents began to fear for their safety.[263] Simply attending school was an act of defiance for girls living in the Taliban-infested Swat Valley in Pakistan. The Taliban is an Islamic terrorist group that, according to the United States Department of State, "aims to overthrow the Government of Pakistan by waging a terrorist campaign against the Pakistani military and state."[264] The Taliban is opposed to Western influence in the Middle East. Particularly, they aim to erase what they view as relics of British colonization in Pakistan, including the country's education system. In January 2009, the group announced its intention to temporarily shut down girl's

---

262 "Malala Yousafazai: Pakistan Activist, 14, Shot in Swat," *BBC*, published October 9, 2012.

263 Ibid.

264 "Country Reports on Terrorism 2016 - Foreign Terrorist Organizations: Tehrik-e Taliban Pakistan (TTP)," United States Department of State, published 19 July 2017.

schools in Swat Valley until the curriculum reflected the Taliban's radical Islamic beliefs.[265]

Many girls continued to attend school in defiance of the Taliban order. This made every minute spent in school an act of rebellion against the Taliban. The bus ride seemed normal, until the bus rounded a curve in the road and slowed down when two strange college-aged boys began approaching the vehicle. They appeared at the open back of the bus, asking the girls, "Who is Malala Yousafzai?"[266] The girls were silent, but they could not help but glance at Malala and then direct their gaze back at the men. That was all the confirmation they needed. One of them proceeded to shoot straight at Malala, firing three times, hitting her in the head and wounding her friends Shazia and Kainat.[267] Malala was rushed to a hospital in Peshawar, Pakistan in critical condition with a bullet dangerously close to her brain.[268] She survived and went on to become one of the world's foremost education and women's rights advocates.

***

Malala Yousafzai is not American, but she embodies the heroic traits inherent to the Rebuilders cohort of Generation Z. It is important to tell her story in this book because she is the most prominent Generation Z activist in the world. She

---

265 Declan Walsh, "Taliban Gun down Girl Who Spoke up for Rights," *New York Times,* October 9, 2012.

266 "Malala Yousafazai: Pakistan Activist, 14, Shot in Swat," BBC, published October 9, 2012.

267 Ibid.

268 Walsh, "Taliban Gun Down Girl."

serves as an inspiration for young people and shows them they are capable of making a difference. Malala, who usually just goes by her first name, has a loud and powerful voice that has transcended language barriers and is now heard across the world.

Malala may not have been a figure on the world stage prior to the brutal attack on her life on that fateful October day, but she was well-known in Pakistan. She began writing an anonymous blog for the BBC when she was just eleven years old that chronicled her experience living in Swat Valley as the region was overtaken by the Taliban.[269] Her father, Ziauddin Yousafzai, operated a school that was among the last schools to educate female students against the orders of the Taliban.[270] In 2009, the school closed and the Yousafzais fled to Abbottabad, Pakistan.[271] Her anonymity began to fade as her profile as an activist rose. Malala continued her work advocating for the rights of women to attend school and was awarded Pakistan's first National Youth Peace Prize in 2011 by Prime Minister Yousaf Raza Gilani; the award has since been named the "National Malala Peace Prize."[272] Malala was also the subject of a 2009 documentary by *The New York Times*.[273] Needless to say, the Taliban took notice.

When her family finally returned to Swat Valley in 2012, Malala went back to school even as her family continued to receive threats from the Taliban. She was undeterred from

---

269 Ibid.
270 Ibid.
271 Ibid.
272 Ibid.
273 Ibid.

her goal of obtaining an education; as she said in her book, "One child, one teacher, one book, one pen can change the world."[274] Her conviction to earn an education and bring attention to the crisis of female education in Pakistan's Swat Valley nearly cost Malala her life.

***

Even though Malala survived the 2012 attack on her life, she is the target of ongoing threats. Ten men were arrested in connection with the attack and two were eventually convicted and sentenced to life in prison.[275] It is unknown whether the gunman who shot Malala was one of the two who were convicted or one of the eight who were acquitted. The acquittal of the eight men who admitted to their involvement in the attack prompted international backlash.[276] Malala's life is still in danger, perhaps even more so due to her high-profile status. For this reason, she has only returned to Pakistan once since her attack.

Malala refused to let the attack and ongoing threats silence her. She has garnered international acclaim for her advocacy work. In 2014, Malala became the youngest person to ever receive the Nobel Peace Prize.[277] She was the first person to represent Gen Z on the international stage and has become the model for the many young activists who now follow in her

274 "Malala Addresses Youth Delegates in UN," UNICEF, published July 12, 2013.

275 Greg Botelho and Aliza Kassim, "Pakistan: 2 Convicted, 8 Acquitted in Connection to Malala Yousafzai Attack," *CNN World*, June 5, 2015.

276 Ibid.

277 "Malala Yousafzai," Nobel Prize, accessed October 23, 2020.

footsteps. She is an inspiration to young women across the globe and has become a feminist icon, meeting with leaders all over the globe to talk about education, human rights, and women's rights. She has spoken out against ISIS, Boko Haram, and the Syrian government.[278]

On her sixteenth birthday, she spoke at the Youth Takeover of the United Nations and said, "Our books and our pens are our most powerful weapons."[279] July 12, her birthday, is now recognized as "Malala Day."[280] From a global perspective, Malala is currently the most influential member of Generation Z. Her personal narrative shows just a sliver of what Gen Zers are capable of achieving when their voices are amplified on the international stage.

278 Ibid.
279 Malala Yousafazi, "Malala Yousafzai: 'Our Books and Our Pens Are the Most Powerful Weapons,'" *The Guardian*, July 12, 2013.
280 "Malala Day," UNESCO, accessed October 23, 2020.

17

THE PARKLAND KIDS

———

This chapter will be examining another crucial event in the formation of Generation Zers political identities: mass shootings. Specifically, the tragic killings at Marjory Stoneman Douglas High School in Parkland, Florida on Valentine's Day of 2018. This event and the subsequent movement of March For Our Lives led by survivors of the shooting served as a political awakening for American teenagers. The brainchild of Parkland survivors, the "Never Again" movement marked the first time Gen Zers had burst onto the American political stage to demand change from the government. The teamwork exhibited by the teenagers who led the movement like Cameron Kasky, Emma Gonzalez, and David Hogg is a clear example of how Gen Zers are living up to their forecasted roles of heroes in the crisis period.

Gun violence in America is an epidemic in and of itself, and the eldest members of Gen Z who compose the cohort I have labeled as the "Rebuilding Generation" are making it a priority in their political lives. The Parkland teenagers demanded that the local, state, and federal governments create stronger gun laws. This was an attempt to influence governmental institutions to act on a critical issue affecting the American public. They also mobilized millions of young people around the world, registered thousands of first-time and young voters, and created an effective social influence campaign in an attempt to revive the civic backbone of America. Their efforts are the result of frustration with ineffective governmental institutions that have failed to protect Americans from gun violence, resulting in a crisis that drove Rebuilders into the streets of American cities in a show of their generation's penchant for heroic action.

Gun violence and mass shootings have become common news items for the Rebuilding Generation, effectively numbing them to the violence while Congress refused to pass concrete reforms to stop it. The shooting at Marjory Stoneman Douglas High School was the straw that broke the camel's back. It helped to shape a shared generational outlook among the eldest Gen Zers that causes them to view gun control as the single most important political issue. This is an issue that comes up not just in my interviews with Gen Zers but has also been a frequent topic of conversation among my friends and classmates for as long as I can remember.

I predict this will be true for decades to come, given that the March For Our Lives was a significant agent of Gen Zers' political socialization. This is due to the fact that it occurred while 1995–2004 babies were in their mid-to-late teens and early twenties, a pivotal time in which their individual political belief system is being cultivated. The teenage activists from Parkland, Florida perfectly encapsulate that part of Strauss and Howe's generational theory that claims that elder Gen Zers will live up to their "hero" label through their ability to team up to navigate America in the midst of a crisis.

***

On Saturday, March 24, 2018, millions of people all over the world took to the streets to demand an end to gun violence at the urging of the Generation Zers who survived the Parkland shooting.[281] Over eight hundred marches were held in cities including London, Paris, Tokyo, Madrid, New York City, Los Angeles, and the main march in Washington, DC.[282] The March For Our Lives and the #NeverAgain movement had gone global. It was the fruit of hundreds of hours of organizing under the direction of Gen Zers.

Nick Roberts had been planning a spring break trip to the nation's capital for months. A "fun coincidence" placed him in the middle of a crowd of hundreds of thousands of people on Pennsylvania Avenue. Over the heads of teens and young adults frustrated with congressional inaction on mass gun violence and beyond the hand-crafted signs screaming for change in bold, Sharpie-d letters, Roberts struggled to see the stage where mass shooting survivors fearlessly stood and stared into the eyes of American history. This was not how he had imagined his spring break trip going, nonetheless he was glad to have found himself in this position.

From a family of gun-owners in America's heartland, Nick Roberts had grown up entrenched in America's distinctive

---

281 Steve Almsay, "March For Our Lives: Top Moments That Made Up A Movement," *CNN*, March 25, 2018.
282 Ibid.

gun culture without being persuaded by its most excessive participants. He does not understand Americans who purchase machine guns, high-capacity magazines, or semi-automatic rifles like the AR-15, which has become infamous as the preferred weapon of mass shooters. Roberts is an advocate for common-sense gun reform like the majority of his generational peers (universal background checks, closing the "gun show loophole"). Before leaving for Washington, DC, he helped organize the March For Our Lives in Indianapolis. Nick Roberts had not yet graduated high school when he helped organize the march. He was not supposed to be at the epicenter of one of the largest social movements in American history; then again, no American student wanted to have to campaign for their own protection against mass shooters.

***

Ethan Block never pictured himself speaking to a crowd of 15,000 people in downtown Philadelphia about gun violence; that is, until Parkland happened. He had grown up in a safe, liberal New Jersey suburb where he was sheltered from the reality of gun violence. Block admits he once felt disconnected from American political reality: "As a sixteen-year-old, upper-class white kid, politics was not something I felt like I needed to care about, so I did not." That sentiment had somewhat shifted after the election of Donald Trump, but like so many other members of Generation Z, Parkland was his true political awakening. What struck him about the shooting was that Parkland had been previously considered to be an extremely safe community not unlike his own. It led him to think, "If it can happen in Parkland, it can happen here." When he heard about the March For Our Lives in DC,

Block was eager to attend. However, he soon realized he had a desire to lead his own march.

Ethan Block first set his sights on nearby Princeton, New Jersey for a march and then realized he wanted to do something bigger, more impactful. In his own words, "I wanted to use my voice, because I knew I had something important to say." His town of Hopewell is not too far from Philadelphia, so he began to meet with gun violence organizations as well as fellow students and activists to organize a march. Ethan Block became the Director of Programming for March For Our Lives in Philadelphia. Soon, he found himself taking interviews with media outlets at lunchtime instead of eating with his classmates in their high school cafeteria.

Block is not one to stay hidden behind the curtain and let his voice go unheard to the masses. He decided he wanted to speak at the march. He had only ever spoken to a crowd as large as thirty people. Still, he knew he had to speak at this rally. His opening acts? Senator Bob Casey and Pennsylvania Attorney General Josh Shapiro. Block describes taking the stage: "Passion fueled me. I started screaming at the top of my lungs and the crowd was going crazy. It was one of the best moments of my life." The work did not stop there. Before the pandemic began, Ethan Block was commuting to Philadelphia every other week to join his fellow March For Our Lives Philadelphia organizers to register voters and plan demonstrations. Block says of his activism, "It has changed my life; I'm not the same person I was before." The March For Our Lives movement across the country had transformed high school students into unlikely activist superstars overnight.

The #NeverAgain movement was born the day after the shooting. Cameron Kasky, a survivor of the shooting at Marjory Stoneman Douglas, invited some friends over to his house after the candlelight vigil to honor their fallen classmates.[283] He had a motive: to start a movement against gun violence spearheaded by students from Marjory Stoneman Douglas.[284] While in the early stages of forming their organization, Kasky posted to his social media: "Stay alert. #NeverAgain."[285] It was a slogan Kasky thought of "while sitting on the toilet in my Ghostbuster pajamas."[286] That same night, the Never Again MSD Facebook page was created.[287] As the organization came into fruition, key members joined the team. Emma Gonzalez, David Hogg, and Jaclyn Corin are just a few of the most recognizable activists who burst onto the national stage in the days following the tragedy in Parkland. Together, the Never Again organization had a unique combination of organizers/mass-mobilizers, fiery orators, and hopeful messengers.

Suddenly, their faces popped up everywhere: CNN, MSNBC, Fox News, ABC, and even the cover of *Time* magazine. The first true test of the movement beyond its commanding social media presence was the national school walkout on

283 Emily Witt, "How the Survivors of Parkland Began the Never Again Movement." *The New Yorker*, February 19, 2018.

284 Ibid.

285 Ibid.

286 Ibid.

287 Ibid.

Wednesday, March 14, 2018.[288] At 10 a.m., I and thousands of other American students got up from our desks and marched out of our school building for seventeen minutes to honor the seventeen lives lost on February 14.[289] It was the first successful showcase of Generation Z's teen activism. The Never Again movement was a culmination of the frustration and grief that an entire generation of American schoolchildren had pent up inside of them.

The activists went on to visit legislatures all over the country, demanding stricter gun control measures. Their tour across the country included dozens of voter registration drives. In the Never Again movement's home state of Florida, youth voter registration increased by 41percent in the two and a half months following the Parkland shooting.[290] They forced NRA-backed Senator Rubio to answer directly to them in a nationally televised town hall.[291] It was the first time Gen Z truly showed their passion for activism and justice with a united front. It was revered as our generation's political awakening. Parkland was the straw that broke the camel's back, we had been awake since the Sandy Hook shooting in 2012 but were too young to understand how the inaction of the government could facilitate it.

The lack of action taken by the federal government to address gun violence in the wake of the murder of twenty-seven

---

288 Jen Kirby, "The National School Walkout, explained," *Vox*, March 14, 2018.

289 Ibid.

290 Alex Daugherty, "Youth Voter Registration Went Up 41 Percent in Florida After Parkland," *Miami Herald*, July 19, 2018.

291 Safia Samee Ali, "Rubio Grilled by Parkland Shooting Survivors, Parents," *NBC News*, February 22, 2018.

people, most of whom were just six and seven years old, continues to anger Rebuilders. As Rebuilders grew older, they realized the full extent of the Sandy Hook shooting. If the murder of innocent first graders was not enough for Congress to pass gun control legislation, many feared it would not happen after the Parkland shooting. The phrase "Never Again" was so poignant because it was not a demand— it was the proposition of a promise that the government had refused to fulfill. The Parkland teens were determined to force the government to promise that what happened in the halls of Columbine High School, Sandy Hook Elementary, Marjory Stoneman Douglas High School, and far too many other schools, bars, clubs, and parks would never happen ever again.

***

"The mass-shooting generation" is another way some experts have referred to Generation Z. It is bleak, but that label does resonate with a generation scarred by the deaths of their generational peers. The oldest of Gen Z were about three years old when two gunmen opened fire in Columbine High School in Colorado on April 20, 1999. The idea that at any moment someone can brandish a gun and open fire is a haunting thought at the back of every Gen Zers mind. We are the generation that were forced to regularly participate in active shooter drills. Sometimes these drills are so realistic that they are traumatizing to the young children who are forced to participate in them.

Even though Baby Boomers were forced to engage in nuclear drills during the Cold War, they never had to wrestle with the reality of watching news footage of a Soviet nuclear bomb being dropped on an American town. Students in schools across the country know the horrific tragedies at Columbine, Sandy Hook, and Parkland all too well. Gen Zers do not know what it is like to feel safe from gun violence in schools. Gen Zers political socialization through these events fostered deep fears of gun violence that influenced the formation of their political belief system. The salience of gun violence in youth political discourse and the palpable fear it evokes in America's children and teens has increased its importance in the eyes of Generation Z, making it a top priority on their political agenda.

***

Every time a lockdown is called, there is no guarantee that it is just a drill. I remember being in elementary school and hearing my principal announce over the PA system that there was "a gift" in the main office. I was too young to understand it, but this was the code my school used to signal we were going into lockdown. In middle school at the end of gym class, we went into lockdown in our locker room. It was a drill, but none of us yet knew that just two hours before that drill, the massacre at Sandy Hook unfolded. I did not find out until I got into my dad's car and he hugged me extra tight. From that day on, he made sure to say to me or text me every single morning before school that he loved me, just in case it was the last thing he said to me. My sister and I both sobbed at mass that weekend when our priest delivered his homily in remembrance of the Sandy Hook victims. I was just twelve years old.

One night when I was in high school, word of an active shooter threat spread throughout social media and group chats. The next day, almost half of the school stayed home at the behest of their concerned parents. I did not stay home. The halls were eerily quiet. In my gym class, it was a meditation day. I could not for the life of me even attempt to relax; instead of meditating, I spent the entire forty minutes listening for noises in the hallway and tensing up at the sound of footsteps approaching the gym. The threat was a false alarm, but it never seemed out of the realm of possibility that it could become reality. At another high school I attended, we went into lockdown because of a possible weapon found on a student. For the hour or more that we sat in the darkness and in stark silence, students had anxiety attacks and frantically texted parents. It turned out that a flashlight had been mistaken for a weapon; nonetheless, it scarred all of us. I thought I had escaped this feeling when I graduated high school.

On Labor Day in 2019, I had another alarming experience. My roommates and I were enjoying a long weekend after the start of our sophomore year of college. Our phones rang with a message from the university. There was an active shooter on campus in one of the freshman dorms. We huddled into a room together, turned off the lights, shoved dressers up against the doors, and shrunk to the ground in silence trying to process what was happening to us. As my friends and I hugged each other for comfort and frantically texted our parents, that same refrain went through my head that Ethan Block, a senior at Hopewell Valley Central High School, articulated: "If it can happen in Parkland, it can happen here." For members of Generation Z, a mass shooting seemed more of an inevitability than a possibility. My dorm was precariously close to the alleged location of the shooter. It was a false alarm, but I had been scarred again.

***

Speak to any Gen Zer about gun violence, and you will hear a similar story. Jacob Pride told me his own story about a shooting threat at his school and came to the same conclusion I did: Gen Zers have a fear that they or someone they love will be a victim of gun violence. When talking about our generation's fear of mass shootings and desire to implement gun control, Tyler Gardner remarked, "The stuff we are trying to change does come from a place of fear, I mean I don't want to get shot and I don't want my friends or siblings to get shot."

Gun violence caused a political awakening for a lot of Gen Zers who realized the only way they could prevent more mass shootings was by turning out to the polls and demanding more from their elected officials. The Parkland kids were a major reason why youth turnout increased drastically in the 2018 midterm elections. John Della Volpe, the polling director for Harvard's Institute of Politics said gun violence is "a central motivating factor in the awakening of this generation, for sure."[292] Of the top sixteen issues most important in America, Della Volpe found "gun violence was in the top five, but school shootings in particular is what stood out for a majority of young Americans."[293] Seventy-seven percent of

292 Brakkton Booker, "After Parkland, Young Voters Were Galvanized, Activists Vow To Continue To Organize," NPR, November 8, 2018.
293 Ibid.

likely young voters said gun control would play a large role in determining their vote in the 2018 midterm elections.[294]

Across the political spectrum, young voters I interviewed supported some kind of gun control measure. Republicans favored universal background checks while Democrats additionally advocated for a national gun owner registry and an assault weapons ban, some even supported a federal gun buyback program. The assault weapons ban has become very popular among likely voters, 67 percent of young Americans who were likely midterm voters in 2018 were supportive of the ban.[295] Gun control has been one of the issues that has seen the largest increase in support in the past decade.

As Generation Z gains more political clout, gun control has become increasingly important in the national policy arena. It is mostly thanks to those teenagers from Parkland, Florida who came together in grief and created a movement that revolutionized the discourse surrounding gun violence in America. They show just what the "heroes" of Generation Z are capable of achieving on the national stage. The students from Marjory Stoneman Douglas created a national movement that showed their generational peers that their voices matter. Their activism inspired others, like Ethan Block, to become politically involved for the first time. The legacy of the March For Our Lives will continue to inspire Generation Zers for the duration of their lifetimes.

---

294 "Harvard IOP Youth Poll Finds Stricter Gun Laws, Ban on Assault Weapons Favored by Two-thirds of Likely Midterm Voters Under Age 30," *Harvard Kennedy School Institute of Politics*, Spring 2018

295 Ibid.

PART V

DEZTINY

18

THE COVID GENERATION

"A date which will live in infamy." This is what President Franklin D. Roosevelt christened December 7, 1941, the day that over three hundred Japanese dive-bombers launched a surprise attack on the US Pacific Fleet at a naval base in Pearl Harbor, Hawaii.[296] More than 2,300 Americans were killed on that fateful day.[297] It was an attack so brazen and a loss so devastating that the United States declared war on Japan, officially entering World War II.[298] On December 9, 2020, just days after the 81st anniversary of the attack on Pearl Harbor, more than 3,400 Americans died of COVID-19 (also referred to as "the coronavirus" or "COVID"), making it one of the deadliest days in American history.[299]

The COVID-19 pandemic is a tragedy of massive proportions. Many Americans have become so desensitized to this

---

296 The Editors of Encyclopaedia Britannica, "Pearl Harbor Attack," *Brittanica*, updated November 30, 2020.

297 Ibid.

298 Ibid.

299 "Trends in Number of COVID-19 Cases and Deaths in the US Reported to CDC, by State/Territory," CDC, accessed January 29, 2021.

tragedy that they are unable to grasp its magnitude. Much like Pearl Harbor and the ensuing tragedy of World War II was a key formative event for young members of the Greatest Generation and elder members of the Silent Generation, the COVID-19 pandemic is poised to serve as the defining event for Generation Z's political and cultural socialization.

This chapter will explore how the pandemic has upended every aspect of Generation Z's formative years of young adulthood and will lead to long-term distrust of governmental and economic institutions. From my own perspective, I will explain what it was like to have "normality" fade instantaneously. This pandemic will impact Gen Z in ways that experts from political, sociological, psychological, and economic fields cannot predict at this moment in time. This chapter will attempt to capture the depth and breadth of the pandemic's immediate effects and what they could mean for the future of the young Americans who grew up during this pandemic.

***

To understand what it is like to be a Gen Zer in this pandemic, we have to go back to the beginning: the week leading up to Friday, March 13, 2020. Yes, it was Friday the 13th. I will walk through my own personal experience of the most tumultuous week of my life. It was one of those surreal moments that one experiences only a few times in their life when they know they are living through a historical moment while it is still unfolding.

Early in the week, just days after returning to campus following spring break, students at my school were notified of the schools' decision to move all classes online for two weeks. As the week slowly unfolded and the NBA canceled their season and celebrities began to contract the coronavirus, the severity of the threat began to sink in. My friends and I fervently discussed whether we should stay on campus or return home for the two weeks while our classes went fully remote. That Wednesday night, I attended a social function with approximately two to three hundred other people, several of whom had, unbeknownst to them at the time, already contracted the virus on their various spring break trips. It was the last normal night of my college life.

Everything declined from that moment on. News of the virus spreading in communities across the nation and a sharp increase in COVID-related deaths sent a shockwave throughout the nation. Colleges began to send students home, word spread that some counties were planning to issue shelter-in-place orders. Americans began to panic. Lysol wipes, hand sanitizer, toilet paper, and paper towels flew off the shelves as people frantically wiped out supermarkets. It was as close as I had ever felt to living in a dystopian nightmare.

Alone in my college apartment, I was preparing for the last weekend before the two-week remote learning period was scheduled to begin when I received a notification: President Trump had issued an emergency declaration in response to the coronavirus. After an anxiety-induced deep clean of my entire living space, I received an email from my university. The entire student body was being kicked off of campus for at least two weeks. I had forty-eight hours to gather my things and leave for an indefinite amount of time. It was Friday the 13th, the day students left their campuses, employees vacated their offices, and an entire nation went into crisis mode. It was the last day I would ever be able to gather with all of my friends in the same room, eat inside with dozens of strangers around me, sit in a classroom less than six feet away from my peers, move about freely without worrying about maintaining social distance, and walk around without a mask covering my nose and mouth. It was the day people cleared grocery store shelves, stocking up on toilet paper and cleaning wipes as if it truly were the end of days.

I had no idea what was to come. All I knew was every student at my university had poured out of their dorm rooms to party like the world was ending. For this reason, my friends and I refer to March 13, 2020 as "the apocalypse." The next morning, I woke up and prayed I had just endured a bad nightmare. At the behest of my parents, I packed up as much of my belongings as I could fit into the suitcases I had at school. My roommates and I left much of our items in our apartment, hoping somehow it would manifest a swift return to campus life. It would be three months before I was allowed back into my room, this time with a mask and gloves on. I passed a temperature check and returned to my dorm with a two-hour window to pack up the remnants of my college life. Now, when I walk the halls of my sophomore year dorm, I am haunted by the memories of my last days of normalcy and all of the memories that could have been made if this pandemic had never happened.

Like so many other Americans, my social life, work life, and education were put on pause while everyone tried to figure out how to adjust to life in a global pandemic. My story is not dissimilar to other Generation Zers who were forced to abruptly abandon their normal way of life. Keith Nagy, who is currently a senior at George Washington University, told me a similar story. He was at a Super Tuesday watch party when he heard several students on his campus were exposed to the coronavirus. Nagy had the foresight to pack up as many of his belongings as possible when he went back to his native Kansas for spring break. It would be months before he returned to the nation's capital.

An overwhelming number of students in the Class of 2020, including my older sister, never got their moment to walk across the stage to receive their diploma. Many Generation Zers entered the workforce at a time when hiring freezes and layoffs prompted record-high unemployment numbers. Many high school seniors mourned the losses of traditions like prom, senior games, and graduation ceremonies while looking toward an uncertain future at colleges that had not yet announced what their fall semesters would look like. The entire nation suffered from a severe case of whiplash as the pandemic upended everything they had ever known.

***

In the early days of the pandemic, Americans rallied to support frontline healthcare workers. In New York City, the initial epicenter of the pandemic, residents opened their windows every night at 7 p.m. to cheer raucously and bang pots and pans to signal their appreciation for doctors and nurses during the day to night shift change.[300] Rallying cries of "Flatten the curve!" united the American public against a common enemy: the exponentially increasing number of COVID-19 cases across the country. Restaurants, retail stores, gyms, and movie theaters closed their doors as several states went into shutdowns to control the spread of cases.[301] Many Americans naively believed that life would be back to "normal" come summertime. As the days went on, tales of hospitals turning away ambulances, frontline healthcare workers reusing surgical masks and making PPE gowns out of garbage bags, and otherwise healthy young Americans fighting for their lives while being hooked up to ventilators made it evident the springtime was only the beginning of this pandemic. It was a marathon, not a sprint.

As desperate and ailing citizens looked to the federal government for leadership, they were met with a storm of disinformation. Just days after declaring a national emergency in response to the coronavirus pandemic, Donald Trump privately told journalist Bob Woodward, "I wanted to always play it down, I still like playing it down, because I don't want to create a panic."[302] Instead of promoting mask-wearing, temporary shutdowns, and social distancing, Trump publicly floated unproven methods of treatment. Among his

300 Lauren M. Johnson, "New York City Spent Two Minutes Clapping for Coronavirus First Responders," *CNN*, March 27, 2020.

301 Moreland et. al, "Timing of State and Territorial COVID-19 Stay-at-Home Orders and Changes in Population Movement—United States, March 1 - May 31, 2020," *Morbidity and Mortality Weekly Report* 69, no. 35 (September 2020), 1198.

302 Jamie Gangel, Jeremy Herb, and Elizabeth Stuart, "'Play It down': Trump Admits to Concealing the True Threat of Coronavirus in New Woodward Book," *CNN*, September 9, 2020.

suggestions were the anti-malaria medication hydroxychloroquine (one Arizona man later died after ingesting it in hopes it would protect him from the virus), exposing patients to large amounts of ultraviolet light, and injecting people with disinfectants like Lysol.[303] Experts predict that if the United States had locked down just one week earlier, tens of thousands of lives could have been saved.[304]

The scale of the loss escalated to the point of it becoming incomprehensible. Many Americans chose to deny the reality of this pandemic rather than confront the tragedy. Americans mourned in private, saying their final goodbyes to family members over FaceTime. Like so many other Americans, I have struggled to reconcile the dual realities of staying home, wearing a mask, and social distancing while scrolling through a social media feed full of friends and influencers alike flouting CDC recommendations. It has been maddening.

I often find myself pondering how I will explain this pandemic to people who did not live through it. It will be difficult for people to wrap their minds around the scale of the loss. Even more difficult in light of the fact that so many people vehemently refused to wear masks, stay at home, limit non-essential travel, and social distance to slow the spread of this virus. Even more difficult when reflecting on the Trump administration's inaction on encouraging these reckless practices. In the meantime, we have all lost over a

303 Dartunorro Clark, "Trump Suggests 'Injection' of Disinfectant to Beat Coronavirus and 'Clean' the Lungs," NBC News, April 23, 2020.
304 James Glanz and Campbell Robertson, "Lockdown Delays Cost at Least 36,000 Lives, Data Shows," The New York Times, May 20, 2020.

year of our "normal" lives to this pandemic. Many of us have lost loved ones, suffered through a COVID-19 infection, and prayed this virus would just go away. In anguish, we have lamented this virus and mourned the lives we once lived.

It is difficult to shake the feeling of having unfinished business to attend to. Like a book with an entire chapter ripped from its spine, the pandemic has created a critical gap in the lives of Generation Zers. In the formative years of their adolescence and young adulthood, they have been ripped from the social environments that normally facilitate their socialization. Outside of the typical classroom structure and the casual environments of school cafeterias, after-school hangouts, parties, and other informal social gatherings, they lack the ability to engage in face-to-face interpersonal discourse. Zoom video chats, FaceTimes, text messages, and virtual classrooms have had to stand-in for these indispensable experiences.

The youngest Gen Zers, who at the time of this book's publication are not yet in middle school, are losing out on crucial developmental experiences. Many of them are attending classes entirely online, missing valuable educational and social opportunities. This pandemic could result in an entire generation of American schoolchildren falling behind in their schoolwork. It is also disproportionately affecting young Americans of Black and Latinx descent, even more so those who come from low-income households. This exacerbates an already large achievement gap between them and their white or more affluent peers. This pandemic has also taken a significant toll on Generation Z's collective mental health.

Growing up in a crisis period, their institutional memory of the American polity is severely impacted by the polarization and instability precipitated by the crisis. In this case, it was a global pandemic with America as the epicenter. It is difficult to articulate how devastating this pandemic is for Gen Zers. For the elder members of Gen Z known as the Rebuilding Generation, they are living through their second economic recession. For young Gen Zers still in middle and high school, their lives are being interrupted at a crucial time for their academic and social development. In the coming years, we will learn just how severely this pandemic affected young Americans. For now, I believe this virus has created an achievement gap that has left millions of students behind in their education and mental development. This pandemic is a form of generational trauma on the scale of a world war.

With no end in sight, the United States remains paralyzed in its fight against this deadly virus. At the time I write this, over 430,000 Americans are dead.[305] An estimated one-third of the entire American population has been infected with COVID-19.[306] Even with vaccine doses being administered across the nation, virus mutations from across the world pose new threats. We do not know when we will go back to "normal." I suspect we will never again return to life exactly as it was before Friday, March 13, 2020. As a generation, we are forever changed by this key historical event.

---

305 "Estimated Disease Burden of COVID-19," CDC, Updated January 19, 2021.
306 Ibid.

This virus has touched every aspect of our lives. We have watched with bated breath as graphs of infections rapidly increased, slowly decreased, and rose back up to a spike once again. We have worn a mask, or sometimes two, whenever we left our household. We have watched nurses and doctors come home from twelve-hour shifts with bruises on their faces from N95 masks. We have stayed six feet apart from strangers in public. We have cried over lost loved ones: friends, family, teachers, and neighbors. We have had swabs stuck up our noses, spit into tubes, and had our blood tested for antibodies. We've felt our hearts sink when a close friend tested positive. We've gone into a two-week quarantine after we were directly exposed to someone who was infected. We've had our temperatures checked at gyms, hair salons, doctor's offices, and stores. We've examined ever-growing lists of symptoms and long-term side effects of infection. We have missed holidays, birthdays, sports games, and graduations. We have watched our favorite restaurants and stores shutter their doors, never to open again. We've washed our hands so much that they bled.

Yet, watching needles push millions of vaccinations into the arms of Americans in an immunological symphony, many Americans cannot help but feel hopeful. One day, hopefully soon, American will emerge from the dark depths of this pandemic. We will materialize as a changed nation, scarred by the losses of our fellow patriots and by the potential long-term effects of COVID-19 infections. We will also remember to never take "normalcy" for granted ever again. We will teach future generations about the pandemic and do our best to ensure the scale of this loss is never replicated again. This generational trauma is meant to teach us lessons: to prioritize public health, mindful leadership, and the common good. Let us go forth with these lessons and keep them at the forefront of our minds as we fulfill our destiny of becoming leaders.

19

WHERE DO WE GO FROM HERE?

———

Demographics are not destiny.

Throughout this book, I have championed the ideals of the youngest voters in the American electorate. The most diverse, progressive Americans to ever take to the voting booths. I have told their stories, of young voters disillusioned by the ideology of aging political parties just now beginning the race to catch up to the rapidly changing American electorate. The stories of young activists taking to the streets to demand a more just and equitable American society. The stories of young Black people aching for racial justice. The stories of schoolchildren grieving for their slain classmates. The stories of politicians answering the call to run for office so that they can represent the next generation of great American leaders.

These stories, although often heartbreaking and conjuring the image of a broken country desperately in need of healing, are tied together by a string of hope. The hope is that the next generation will be better, will rise to the challenge of bringing this country closer to the ideal of equal protection under law for all of its inhabitants as enshrined in the living, breathing document that is the United States Constitution. It is a vision of an America that is accepting of all people, no matter their skin color, country of origin, religion, sexuality, gender identity, or socioeconomic class. It is a vision often written off as naive, too proximate to utopian, and simply unattainable.

It is not foolish to have hope; it is necessary when constructing a vision of a better America. A professor once said to me, "You strung a narrative together and then said, 'Hopefully.' We have to stop using 'hopefully' and start being strategic." While I see the value of prioritizing strategy over hopefulness, the former does not exist without the latter. Hope is what drives us. In the absence of hope, we have nothing except fear. Dare I say that in the absence of hope we have ideologies proximate to Trumpism. We have demagoguery, fear mongering, and civil unrest. It is undeniable that fear is a powerful motivating force, but what one gets from fear is resistance, not progress.

When I say hope, I mean that we believe in a better vision for America, one that looks forward, to right wrongs and facilitate justice, and not backward. It is a vision that embraces the ever-changing nature of the demographics of this country yet never loses sight of our democratic ideals, one that seeks to include, not exclude. This vision challenges us to undertake the hard work of creating systems that bring us closer to realizing the ideal of all Americans having the ability to pursue life, liberty, and the pursuit of happiness. It encourages us to expand access to opportunities for upward mobility like higher education, quality healthcare, equal access to housing, and equal opportunities for employment.

When I wrote the bulk of this book, I had no idea what would happen in the 2020 election and the events that would ensue in the following weeks. The young people I talked to and the extensive research I was engaged in for several months all pointed me toward my prediction that Donald Trump would be defeated. His agenda, which is farther to the right than any form of traditional conservatism, does not align with the future trajectory of American politics. Trumpism cannot survive the rising tide of a young, diverse American electorate.

From my research, I was convinced the Republican Party would no longer be the party of Trump if they wanted to maintain electoral viability in the coming decade; however, it was evident that he would not go down without a fight. This is what I knew. I could not have predicted the events of the final days of Donald Trump's presidency. I could not have predicted an armed insurrection directly incited by Donald Trump in which thousands of his supporters breached the Capitol building while every senator and representative, and the vice president, were inside the building certifying the 2020 election results.[307] I could not have predicted several people would die that day and that these supporters would be carrying flex cuffs, tasers, and handguns in an effort to take elected officials hostage and publicly lynch them.[308] I

307 David Leonhardt, "Inside the Capitol Attack," *The New York Time*, January 19, 2021.
308 Ellina Abovian, "From Plastic Zip-Tie Handcuffs to Pipe Bombs, Sinister Nature of Assault on the Capitol Is Coming into Focus," *KTLA*, January

could not have predicted that he would be the first American president to be impeached twice.[309]

In the final days of his presidency, it is no wonder so many of the president's former allies turned on him. While exhibiting all of the classic features of an emerging autocrat throughout his tenure in office, Trump somehow managed to push American democracy to the brink of collapse without being removed from office. He laid the groundwork from his earliest days of peddling the birtherism conspiracy theory about Barack Obama, to gaslighting the American public during his Presidency by lying about everything from the size of his inaugural crowd to the severity of the global coronavirus pandemic.[310]

In his final days of power, Trump indulged the very worst impulses of his supporters by promulgating conspiracies about the 2020 elections and riling them up to overtake the federal government.[311] After his supporters launched an insurrection effort directly incited by the President's own false rhetoric surrounding his electoral loss, it finally became apparent to most Senate and House Republicans that Trump was not the man who they should build the future of their

11, 2021.

309 Nicholas Fandos, "Trump Impeached for Inciting Insurrection," *The New York Times*, January 13, 2021

310 The Washington Post Fact Checker, "In Four Years, President Trump Made 30,573 False or Misleading Claims," *The Washington Post*, updated January 20, 2021.

311 Jonathan Swan and Zachary Basu, "Episode 8: The Siege," *Axios*, January 21, 2021.

party around.[312] In the Trump era, the United States came the closest it has ever come to a complete breakdown of its democratic institutions. Yet the most awesome power afforded to the Senate by the country's Founding Fathers, the ability to convict a president and bar him from holding office, was not triggered.

***

As a new administration comes into power, there will be new opportunities for young people to advance their political agenda. Joe Biden is by no means a perfect candidate, but he embodied the same hope and change that his partner in governance, Barack Obama, offered to the nation in 2008. Much like Obama, President Biden inherits a nation deep in the throes of an economic disaster. He also faces a pandemic, escalating threats of domestic terrorism, racial strife, and the time-sensitive climate crisis.[313] President Biden faces an uphill battle that America cannot afford for him to lose.

After his inauguration on January 20, 2021, Joe Biden became the oldest sitting president in American history.[314] Born in 1942, Biden is a member of the Silent Generation which spans the years 1928–1945.[315] He is the first, and will also likely be the last, president from the Silent Generation. In Washington,

---

312 Gabriel Sherman, "'They're Being Told to Stay Away from Trump': After a Day of Violence and 25th Amendment Chatter, Trump's Allies Are Jumping Ship," *Vanity Fair,* January 7, 2021.

313 Reid Wilson, "Biden Faces 100 Days of Crisis," *The Hill,* January 20, 2021.

314 Johnny Diaz, "Biden Is the Oldest President to Take the Oath," *The New York Times,* January 18, 2021.

315 Dan Zak, "Joe Biden, 78, Will Lead an American Gerontocracy," *The Washington Post,* January 12, 2021

he is surrounded by his generational peers: President Pro Tempore of the United States Senate Patrick Leahy, Senate Minority Leader Mitch McConnell, and President Pro Tempore emeritus of the United States Senate Chuck Grassley are all members of the Silent Generation as well.[316] Yet the median age of a United States resident is 38.2.[317] Joe Biden has billed himself as a "transition candidate."[318] That transition may very well be a shift of power from elder Americans to young generations ready and willing to take up the mantle of governance. Biden may be the one to right the ship, but who will take the wheel when he steps aside?

When Amanda Gorman, who at just twenty-two years old become the youngest inaugural poet, delivered her poem "The Hill We Climb" atop the steps to the US Capitol at President Biden's inauguration, she highlighted the relationships between American generations.[319] Gorman spoke these words:

A country that is bruised, but whole. Benevolent, but bold. Fierce and free. We will not be turned around or interrupted by intimidation, Because we know our inaction and inertia will be the inheritance of

---

316 Paul Kane, "Senate's Octogenarians Face the Age Question and Whether It's Time to Exit," *The Washington Post*, December 12, 2020.

317 Luke Rogers, "Counties Can Have the Same Median Age but Very Different Population Distributions," *United States Census Bureau*, June 20, 2019.

318 Diaz, "Biden Is the Oldest President."

319 Zoe Christen Jones, "Amanda Gorman Reads 'the Hill We Climb' at Biden's Inauguration," *CBS News*, January 21, 2021.

the next generation. Our blunders become their burdens. But one thing is certain, if we merge mercy with might and might with the right, Then love becomes our legacy and change our children's birthright. So let us leave behind the country better than the one we were left, With every breath in my bronze-pounded chest, We will raise this wounded world into a wondrous one.[320]

—AMANDA GORMAN

A Gen Zer herself, Gorman drew attention to the ways in which our democratic institutions and their leaders are connected throughout history. The dichotomy between the youngest inaugural poet ever presenting this vision of America and the swearing in of the oldest president in United States history was glaringly apparent in a way that made it purposeful. It was a presentation of hope that there will be young Americans to take the wheel and steer the ship.

In the twenty in-depth interviews I conducted with members of Gen Z's activist class for this book, the penultimate question I asked was, "In your political life, do you believe that you are driven more by hope or by fear?" Only two of them said fear. Eighteen of them said hope. While they did not deny there are many things to be afraid of at this particular moment in history, it is hope that keeps them going. I believe Keith Nagy summed it up best when he told me, "I

---

320 Ibid.

don't discount the fact that fear is an incredibly motivating factor.... People can capitalize on that fear. But I would choose to believe that people are good at heart, and I know that our politics can be more sincere and optimistic." There are no strategies to strengthen our democracy without the hope that our country can realize the idyllic vision that the Founding Fathers had for their young nation.

It is through hope we create strategies to increase the representation of minority groups in the government who can advance agendas that give all minority groups access to these opportunities for upward mobility. When I say we have to let hope guide us here, I mean we have to believe in the cyclical nature of American history. We have to realize the nature of politics is that new generations replace older ones as leaders and advance the issues that matter the most to them. As they continue to gain a larger share of the electorate and begin to outnumber the Silent Generation, Baby Boomers, and even Gen Xers, Rebuilders hold the keys to leadership of the free world. It is incumbent on all Americans to invest in these young Americans and to recognize the promise they hold. The promise of a more diverse, equitable American society.

***

On the last day of the Constitutional Convention in 1787, many Americans gathered outside of Independence Hall in Philadelphia. When the framers exited the building after adopting the Constitution, Elizabeth Willing Powel asked Benjamin Franklin, "What do we have, a republic or a monarchy?" to which Franklin famously replied, "A republic, if you can keep it."[321]

When it comes their turn, it will be Generation Zers who are the keepers of this republic. They will be the ones who assume the highest offices in the land and outline their concrete policy platforms to address the issues that matter to them. This includes, but is not limited to racial justice, climate change, higher education access, gun control, healthcare, criminal justice reform and income inequality. This is the reckoning that we are approaching. It does not have to be scary; it is the nature of political evolution. A power shift from the old back to the young that has historically occurred throughout American history to keep our nation moving forward. It is the Rebuilders who are facilitating this transition. Taking to the streets, questioning lawmakers, educating themselves on issues like mass incarceration, redlining, the collapse of the middle class, environmental racism, and food deserts.

The young people that have been featured in this book feel the weight of the country's future on their shoulders. They are ready to rise to the challenge. While demographics are not destiny, they are the ballgame when it comes to politics. Politics is ultimately a game of numbers, of calculations that are made in order to be victorious. When young people take to the voting booth, they are factored into these calculations. Politics is a virtuous cycle that rewards those who show up. If we show up, the issues we care about rise to the forefront of the nation's collective political consciousness. Each one of

---

321 Zara Anishanslin, "What We Get Wrong about Ben Franklin's 'A Republic, If You Can Keep It,'" *The Washington Post,* October 29, 2019.

us is therefore called to participate in democracy, to uphold the democratic ideals of this nation, and leave America as a better nation for our children than it was for us.

Our nation is at a crossroads, and it will largely be up to young people to decide what course this country takes over the next two decades as we enter the next cycle of American history. As we emerge from a global pandemic, confront a racial reckoning, and chart the course of the next two decades, it is up to young people to realize the vision of a more just and equitable American society that they have constructed throughout the narratives in this book. It may sound radical at first, but it is not. This is simply the next step in the pattern of American history. Like every other generation before us, we will prioritize the issues and values that matter to us and create systems that advance them when we are given the chance.

When I say that demographics are not destiny, I mean we cannot realize our collective vision without being given the opportunity to have our voices heard. Generation Z cannot succeed if we are continuously discounted. If we are to carry the torch, it has to be passed to us. We are ready and willing to steer the ship, to carry the torch, and to be the keepers of a fragile, yet resilient, American democracy.

ACKNOWLEDGMENTS

This book would not have been published without the help of everyone at the Creator Institute and New Degree Press. Thank you to Professor Eric Koester, who jumpstarted this publishing journey. Thank you to my developmental editor, Adam Burkhart, my acquiring editor, Jen Wichman, and my marketing and revisions editor, Bianca DaSilva, for helping this book realize its full potential. Thank you also to the publishing team and author's coaches at New Degree Press, especially Brian Bies, for helping this first-time author through the process of marketing and publishing a book.

I also could not have written this book without the constant love and support of my family. Thank you to my dad Jim Lambert and my mom Janet Lambert. The best thing in the world is being your daughter. Thank you to my sister Rachel Lambert for encouraging me to continue with this project on the days where I wanted to give up. I am fortunate to count my loving grandparents among my biggest supporters. To Jim Lambert ("Pop Pop Jim"), Dawne Anderson Lambert, Peggy Wyllie ("Nommy"), and Rita Stutzman ("Mama Ree"),

I cannot thank you enough. Thank you to my cousin, Victoria Wyllie, who is more like a sister to me.

Thank you also to my friends who have stuck with me through this process. To my roommates Alicia Casciano, Jane Harris, and Daniella LaPorta, thank you for providing me with endless love and support throughout this journey. To my friends Olivia Bassetti, Christina Carrozza, Kamryn Dow, Ali Leen, Tom Rafter, Nick Weichel, and Jake Zisa, thank you for always believing in me and this project.

Thank you to everyone I interviewed for this book, including Ethan Block, Noah Fenstermacher, Tyler Gardner, Alex Joshua, Aly Kotelnicki, Gracie Smith, Jacob Pride, Nick Roberts, Ryan Wolfe, and many more Gen Zers who you will get to know through the stories in this book.

Thank you to my AP Government and Politics teacher, Brooke Oels, who ignited my passion for political science. Thank you to my AP Language and Composition teacher, Randy Koetzner, for showing me the power of good writing. Thank you to Professor Karen Graziano who convinced me my words were powerful. Thank you to Dr. Wesley Proctor who is living proof that one person can change the world. Thank you to Dr. Allyson Levin for teaching me that the messages we choose to share with the world matter. Thank you to Dean Adele Lindenmeyr for creating an educational environment that makes me proud to be a Villanovan.

Thank you to the young activists who inspired this book. It has been the honor of my lifetime to immortalize the stories of our generation in this book.

Thank you to everyone who contributed to the pre-launch campaign for this book: Adam Niedbalski, Aman Shah, Amy Beversluis, Amy Deutschmeister, Andrea Tannenbaum, Angela B. Thompson, Anne Rogalin, Barbara Lewis, Bob Lutkewitte, Brian Kopnicki, Carol Regal, Carolyn Skowron, Christopher Matthew, Conor Darken, David Mason, Donna Dillon, Elena Trentacoste, Emily Wyrwa, Gene Graf, Hannah Sage, Jay Joseph, Jill Carter, Joe Compagnia, Kalpana Krishna-Kumar, Karen Bassetti, Kata Blazejewski, Kathleen Porter, Kathy McLoughlin, Kelly Weigle, Kevin Boris, Kim Jacks, Lauren Rogalin, Marcia Abey, Mary Woodward, MaryAnn Maidl, Matthew Fagerstrom, Matthew Swenson, Melinda Willson, Meredith White, Michael Bassetti, Michael Caro, Michelle Ferrer, Mike Morreale, Miles Coleman, Nancy Peralta, Nia Rainer, Nicole Fiorita, Nicole Harris, Nicole Hudson, Nicole Vuono, Noreen Brown, Paul Schwartz, Rachel Graham, Rachel Rojek, Rebecca Reed, Regina Regan, Richard Lippert, Rob Slifer, Robert Cantwell, Robert Kellert, Robert McCoid, Samuel Goodman, Sara Barshap, Shafuq Naseem, Shelly Hart, Shirley Abel, Stan Fryczynski, Stefanie Tavaglione, Stephanie Wollman, Tracy Flack Tyler, Trinity Hart, Tyler Crotty, Vikram Kapoor, and William Clifton. This book would not have been possible without your support.

APPENDIX

WINTER

Beadle, Kelly, Ruby Belle Booth, Alison Cohen, Peter de Guzman, Bennett Fleming Wood, Noorya Hayat, Kei Kawashima-Ginsberg, Sarah Keese, Abby Kiesa, Rey Junco, Kathleen Lanzilla, Kristian Lundberg, Alberto Medina, and Lauren Soherr. "Election Week 2020: Young People Increase Turnout, Lead Biden to Victory." *Tuft University Center for Information and Research on Civic Learning and Engagement*, November 25, 2020. https://circle.tufts.edu/latest-research/election-week-2020#youth-voter-turnout-increased-in-2020.

Gould, Elise. "Decades of Rising Economic Inequality in the U.S.." *Economic Policy Institute*, March 27, 2019. https://www.epi.org/publication/decades-of-rising-economic-inequality-in-the-u-s-testimony-before-the-u-s-house-of-representatives-ways-and-means-committee/.

Hansen, Claire. "Young Voters Turned Out in Historic Numbers, Early Estimates Show." *U.S. News*, November 7, 2018. https://

www.usnews.com/news/politics/articles/2018-11-07/young-voters-turned-out-in-historic-numbers-early-estimates-show.

Harvard Kennedy School Institute of Politics. "Harvard Youth Poll: Election 2020." Published October 26, 2020. https://iop.harvard.edu/youth-poll/harvard-youth-poll.

Hedgeye. "The Fourth Turning: Why American 'Crisis' May Last Until 2030." April 1, 2017. YouTube Video, 14:42. https://www.youtube.com/watch?v=8Yfb2zQjKWE.

Lorenz, Taylor. "Hype House and the Los Angeles TikTok Mansion Gold Rush." *The New York Times,* January 3, 2020. https://www.nytimes.com/2020/01/03/style/hype-house-los-angeles-tik-tok.html.

Parker, Kim, and Ruth Igielnik. "On the Cusp of Adulthood and Facing an Uncertain Future: What We Know about Gen Z So Far." *Pew Research Center,* May 14, 2020. https://www.pewsocialtrends.org/essay/on-the-cusp-of-adulthood-and-facing-an-uncertain-future-what-we-know-about-gen-z-so-far/.

Strauss, William, and Neil Howe. *The Fourth Turning: An American Prophecy - What the Cycles of History Tell Us About America's Next Rendezvous with Destiny.* New York: Crown, 2009.

University of Minnesota Libraries. "Political Socialization." Accessed January 5, 2020.

Witt, Emily. "How the Survivors of Parkland Began the Never Again Movement." *The New Yorker,* February 19, 2018. https://

www.newyorker.com/news/news-desk/how-the-survivors-of-parkland-began-the-never-again-movement.

ZBELLION

Agustin, Bianca, Chuck Collins, Jonathan Heller, Sara Myklebust, and Omar Ocampo. *Billionaire Wealth vs. Community Health: Protecting Essential Workers.* Washington, D.C.: Institute for Policy Studies, 2020. https://inequality.org/wp-content/uploads/2020/11/Report-Billionaires-EssentialWorkers-FINAL.pdf.

Barro, Josh. "3 Big Economic Trends of the 2010s." *New York Magazine*, December 30, 2019. https://nymag.com/intelligencer/2019/12/3-big-economic-trends-of-the-2010s.html.

Manduca, Robert. "Income Inequality and the Persistence of Racial Economic Disparities." *Sociological Science* 5, no. 3 (March 2018). https://doi.org/10.15195/v5.a8.

Parker, Kim, and Ruth Igielnik. "On the Cusp of Adulthood and Facing an Uncertain Future: What We Know about Gen Z So Far." *Pew Research Center*, May 14, 2020. https://www.pewsocialtrends.org/essay/on-the-cusp-of-adulthood-and-facing-an-uncertain-future-what-we-know-about-gen-z-so-far/.

Seemiller, Corey, and Meghan Grace. *Generation Z: A Century in the Making.* New York: Routledge, 2019.

Turse, Nick. "Pentagon War Game Includes Scenario for Military Response to Domestic Gen Z Rebellion." *The Intercept*, June

5, 2020. https://theintercept.com/2020/06/05/pentagon-war-game-gen-z/.

THE HOMELAND GEN

Howe, Neil. "Introducing the Homeland Generation." *Forbes*, October 27, 2014. https://www.forbes.com/sites/neilhowe/2014/10/27/introducing-the-homeland-generation-part-1-of-2/#4c0920f-c2bd6.

Pew Research Center. "The Generation Gap in American Politics." *Pew Research*, March 1, 2018. https://www.pewresearch.org/politics/2018/03/01/3-u-s-foreign-policy-and-americas-global-standing-islam-and-violence-nafta/.

Seemiller, Corey, and Meghan Grace. *Generation Z: A Century in the Making*. New York: Routledge, 2019.

Thrall, Trevor, Dina Smeltz, Erik Goepner, Will Ruger, and Craig Kafura. "The Clash of Generations? Intergenerational Change and American Foreign Policy Views." *The Chicago Council on Global Affairs*, June 25, 2018.

https://www.thechicagocouncil.org/publication/clash-generations-intergenerational-change-and-american-foreign-policy-views.

MEDIA LITERACY

The Associated Press. "Trump Picks Tulsa on Juneteenth for Return to Rallies." *NBC News*, June 10, 2020. https://www.

nbcnews.com/politics/donald-trump/trump-picks-tulsa-june-teenth-return-campaign-rallies-n1229681.

Conger, Kate, and Mike Isaac. "Twitter Permanently Bans Trump, Capping Online Revolt." *The New York Times*, January 10, 2020. https://www.nytimes.com/2021/01/08/technology/twitter-trump-suspended.html.

Lorenz, Taylor, Kellen Browning, and Sheera Frenkel. "TikTok Teens and K-Pop Stans Say They Sank Trump Rally." *The New York Times*, June 21, 2020. https://www.nytimes.com/2020/06/21/style/tiktok-trump-rally-tulsa.html.

Marantz, Andrew. "How New Jersey's Twitter Found Its 'Big State Energy.'" *The New Yorker*, January 20, 2020. https://www.newyorker.com/magazine/2020/01/20/how-new-jerseys-twitter-found-its-big-state-energy.

Messer, Chris M., Thomas E. Shriver, and Alison E. Adams. "The Destruction of Black Wall Street: Tulsa's 1921 Riot and the Eradication of Accumulated Wealth." *Am J Econ Sociol* 77, no. 3-4 (May-September 2018): 789-819. https://doi.org/10.1111/ajes.12225.

Mueller, Robert S. III. *The Mueller Report*. Washington D.C.: U.S. Department of Justice, 2019.

Orlowski, Jeff, dir. *The Social Dilemma*. Written by Davis Coombe, Vickie Curtis, and Jeff Orlowski, featuring Tristan Harris. Produced by Exposure Labs. Los Gatos, CA: Netflix, 2020.

Rosenberg, Matthew, Nicholas Confessore, and Carole Cadwalladr. "How Trump Consultants Exploited the Facebook Data of Millions." *The New York Times,* March 17, 2018. https://www.nytimes.com/2018/03/17/us/politics/cambridge-analytica-trump-campaign.html.

Soloman, Dan. "Beto O'Rourke's Endless Livestream." *Texas Monthly,* November 12, 2018. https://www.texasmonthly.com/the-culture/beto-orourkes-endless-livestream/.

Stewart, Emily. "Lawmakers Seem Confused about What Facebook Does- and How They Do It." *Vox,* April 10, 2018. https://www.vox.com/policy-and-politics/2018/4/10/17222062/mark-zuckerberg-testimony-graham-facebook-regulations.

Tiffany, Kaitlyn. "You Can't Buy Memes," *The Atlantic,* February 28, 2020. https://www.theatlantic.com/technology/archive/2020/02/bloomberg-memes-instagram-ads/607219/.

Voght, Kara. "The Memeable Mr. Markey." *Mother Jones,* August 26, 2020. https://www.motherjones.com/politics/2020/08/the-memeable-mr-markey/.

Williams, Christine B., and Girish J. "Jeff" Gulati. "Digital Advertising Expenditures in the 2016 Presidential Election." *Social Science Computer Review* 36, no. 4 (August 2018): 406–21. https://doi.org/10.1177/0894439317726751.

GEN Z AND RACE

Barroso, Amanda. "Gen Z Eligible Voters Reflect the Growing Racial and Ethnic Diversity of U.S. Electorate." *Pew Research*

Center, September 23, 2020. https://www.pewresearch.org/fact-tank/2020/09/23/gen-z-eligible-voters-reflect-the-growing-ra-cial-and-ethnic-diversity-of-u-s-electorate/

Eligon, John, and Audra D.S. Burch. "Black Voters Helped Deliver Biden a Presidential Victory. Now What?" *The New York Times*, November 11, 2020. https://www.nytimes.com/2020/11/11/us/joe-biden-black-voters.html.

Finucane, Martin. "6 Things to Know About Rev. Raphael Warnock and Jon Ossoff." *The Boston Globe*, January 6, 2021. https://www.bostonglobe.com/2021/01/06/nation/6-things-know-about-rev-raphael-warnock-jon-ossoff/.

Grigsby Bates, Karen. "A Look Back at Trayvon Martin's Death, and the Movement It Inspired." *NPR*, July 31, 2018. https://www.npr.org/sections/codeswitch/2018/07/31/631897758/a-look-back-at-trayvon-martins-death-and-the-movement-it-inspired.

Jackson, Andrew P., Denyvetta Davis, and Jason Kelly Alston. "Remotivating the Black Vote: The Effect of Low-Quality Information on Black Voters in the 2016 Presidential Election and How Librarians Can Intervene." *The Library Quarterly* 87, no. 3 (July 2017), 237. https://doi.org/10.1086/692300.

Miami Herald. "A Look at What Happened the Night Trayvon Martin Died." *The Tampa Bay Times*, July 6, 2012. https://www.tampabay.com/news/publicsafety/crime/a-look-at-what-hap-pened-the-night-trayvon-martin-died/1223083/.

Parker, Kim, and Ruth Igielnik. "On the Cusp of Adulthood and Facing an Uncertain Future: What We Know about Gen Z So

Far." *Pew Research Center*, May 14, 2020. https://www.pewsocialtrends.org/essay/on-the-cusp-of-adulthood-and-facing-an-uncertain-future-what-we-know-about-gen-z-so-far/.

Slodysko, Brian. "Explainer: How Democrats Won Georgia's 2 Senate Runoffs." *AP News*, January 6, 2021. https://apnews.com/article/associated-press-georgia-election-result-60954fd7d3d3b6b49a8884c0c026247d.

Smith, Ben, and Byron Tau. "Birtherism: Where It All Began." *Politico*, April 22, 2011. https://www.politico.com/story/2011/04/birtherism-where-it-all-began-053563.

Stockman, Farah, and John Eligon. "Cities Ask if It's Time to Defund Police and 'Reimagine' Public Safety," *The New York Times*, June 5, 2020. https://www.nytimes.com/2020/06/05/us/defund-police-floyd-protests.html.

Thebault, Reis, Michael Scherer, and Cleve R. Wootson Jr. "Raphael Warnock Wins Georgia Runoff Election Against Sen. Loeffler, Lifting Democratic Hopes of Claiming Senate Majority." *The Washington Post*, January 6, 2021. https://www.washingtonpost.com/politics/perdue-ossoff-loeffler-warnock-georgia-senate/2021/01/05/7d7b5afe-4f5d-11eb-83e3-322644d82356_story.html.

THE PROUD GENERATION

Asakura, Kenta. "Extraordinary Acts to 'Show Up': Conceptualizing Resilience of LGBTQ+ Youth." *Youth & Society* 51, no. 2 (March 2019), 268-285. https://doi.org/10.1177/0044118X16671430.

Biden-Harris Transition. "President-Elect Biden Announces Mayor Pete Buttigieg as Nominee for Secretary of Transportation." Updated December 15, 2020. https://buildbackbetter.gov/press-releases/president-elect-biden-announces-mayor-pete-buttigieg-as-nominee-for-secretary-of-transportation/.

Johns, Andrew L., ed. *A Companion To Ronald Reagan.* Chichester, UK: Wiley Blackwell, 2015.

Deckman, Melissa, and Mileah Kromer. "Young LGBT Americans Are More Politically Engaged Than the Rest of Generation Z." *The Conversation*, June 28, 2019. https://theconversation.com/young-lgbt-americans-are-more-politically-engaged-than-the-rest-of-generation-z-119506.

Imse, Elliot. "The Rainbow Wave May Touch Down in State Legislatures." *Victory Fund*, November 5, 2018. https://victoryfund.org/the-rainvow-wave-may-touch-down-in-state-legislatures/.

Allister, Graeme. *JWT: Generation Z- Executive Summary.* New York: J. Walter Thompson Intelligence, May 2019. https://www.slideshare.net/jwtintelligence/jwt-generation-z-48070734.

Kacala, Alexander. "Michelle Obama Reveals She Snuck Out of White House to Celebrate Gay Marriage Ruling." *NBC News*, November 16, 2018. https://www.nbcnews.com/feature/nbc-out/michelle-obama-reveals-she-snuck-out-white-house-celebrate-gay-n937186.

McInroy, Lauren B., and Shelley L. Craig. "Perspectives of LGBTQ Emerging Adults on the Depiction and Impact of LGBTQ

Media Representation." *Journal of Youth Studies* 20, no. 1 (2017), 32-46. https://doi.org/10.1080/13676261.2016.1184243.

Mukherjee, Siddartha. *The Emperor of All Maladies: A Biography of Cancer.* New York: Scribner, 2011.

Obergefell v. Hodges, 576 U.S. 644 (2015).

Parker, Kim, and Ruth Igielnik. "On the Cusp of Adulthood and Facing an Uncertain Future: What We Know about Gen Z So Far." *Pew Research Center,* May 14, 2020. https://www.pewsocialtrends.org/essay/on-the-cusp-of-adulthood-and-facing-an-uncertain-future-what-we-know-about-gen-z-so-far/.

Pew Research Center. "Attitudes on Same Sex Marriage." Published May 14, 2019. https://www.pewforum.org/fact-sheet/changing-attitudes-on-gay-marriage/.

Republican National Committee. "Resolution Regarding the Republican Party Platform." published August 24, 2020. https://prod-cdn-static.gop.com/media/documents/RESOLUTION_REGARDING_THE_REPUBLICAN_PARTY_PLATFORM.pdf?_ga=2.109560193.504857691.1598219603-2087748323.1598219603.

Stelter, Brian. "Campaign Offers Help to Gay Youths." *The New York Times,* October 18, 2010. https://www.nytimes.com/2010/10/19/us/19video.html.

Vandermaas-Peeler, Alex, Daniel Cox, Molly Fisch-Friedman, and Robert P. Jones. "Diversity, Division, Discrimination: The State of Young America." *Public Religion Research Institute,* January

10, 2018. https://www.prri.org/research/mtv-culture-and-religion/.

Wax-Thibodeaux, Emily. "Biden's Ambitious LGBT Agenda Poises Him to Be Nation's Most Pro-Equality President in History." January 11, 2021. https://www.washingtonpost.com/politics/2021/01/11/biden-lgbtq-policies/.

PETE FOR AMERICA

ABC Democratic Debate. Moderated by George Stephanopoulos, David Muir, and Linsey Davis. Aired February 7, 2020, on ABC.

Biden-Harris Transition. "President-Elect Biden Announces Mayor Pete Buttigieg as Nominee for Secretary of Transportation." Published December 15, 2020. https://buildbackbetter.gov/press-releases/president-elect-biden-announces-mayor-pete-buttigieg-as-nominee-for-secretary-of-transportation/.

DeCosta-Klipa, Nik. "Pete Buttigieg Explains Why He Didn't Come Out Until Nearly His Second Term as South Bend Mayor." Boston.com, April 3, 2019. https://www.boston.com/news/politics/2019/04/03/pete-buttigieg-gay-coming-out.

Hicks, Michael J. "An Indiana Economist Looks at South Bend's Revival Under Buttigieg." MarketWatch, April 19, 2019. https://www.marketwatch.com/story/an-indiana-economist-looks-at-south-bends-revival-under-pete-buttigieg-2019-04-12.

Della Volpe, John. "The Role of Young Voters in 2020." Interview by Kerri Miller, *MPR News with Kerri Miller,* MPR News, April 27, 2020, audio, 50:02.

Pete Buttigieg. Interview by Trevor Noah. *The Daily Show with Trevor Noah.* February 6, 2020. https://www.youtube.com/watch?v=r6jOokwPMDE.

Rodriguez, Barbara. "Pete Buttigieg Made History in the Iowa Caucuses Whatever the Final Results Show." *Des Moines Register,* February 5, 2020. https://www.desmoinesregister.com/story/news/elections/presidential/caucus/2020/02/05/pete-buttigieg-first-openly-gay-candidate-earn-presidential-primary-delegates-nomination/4667796002/.

Schneider, Elena. "Buttigieg Drops Out of Presidential Race." *Politico,* March 1, 2021. https://www.politico.com/news/2020/03/01/buttigieg-dropping-out-of-presidential-race-118489.

Zurcher, Anthony. "Pete Buttigieg: How a Young, Gay Mayor Became a Democratic Star." *BBC News,* April 9, 2019. https://www.bbc.com/news/world-us-canada-47860012.

YOUNG REPUBLICANS

Al Jazeera Staff. "Who is Who in the Trump Caucus? Are They the Republican Future?" *Al Jazeera,* January 15, 2021. https://www.aljazeera.com/news/2021/1/15/whos-who-in-the-trump-caucus-are-they-the-republican-future.

Cai, Weiya, Annie Daniel, Lazaro Gamio, and Alicia Parlapiano. "Impeachment Results: How Democrats and Republicans

Voted." *The New York Times*, January 13, 2021. https://www.nytimes.com/interactive/2021/01/13/us/politics/trump-second-impeachment-vote.html.

Harvard Kennedy School Institute of Politics. "Harvard Youth Poll." Published April 23, 2020. https://iop.harvard.edu/youthpoll/harvard-youth-poll.

Heath, Brad, and Sarah N. Lynch. "U.S. Says Capitol Rioters Meant to 'Capture and Assassinate' Officials - Filing." *Reuters*, January 15, 2021. https://www.reuters.com/article/us-usa-trump-capitol-arrests/u-s-says-capitol-rioters-meant-to-capture-and-assassinate-officials-filing-idUSKBN29K0K7.

Della Volpe, John. "The Role of Young Voters in 2020." Interview by Kerri Miller, *MPR News with Kerri Miller*, MPR News, April 27, 2020, audio, 50:02.

Parker, Kim, Nikki Graf, and Ruth Igielnik. "Generation Z Looks a Lot Like Millennials on Key Social and Political Issues." *Pew Research Center*, January 17, 2019. https://www.pewsocialtrends.org/2019/01/17/generation-z-looks-a-lot-like-millennials-on-key-social-and-political-issues/.

Republican National Committee. "Resolution Regarding the Republican Party Platform." Published August 24, 2020. https://prod-cdn-static.gop.com/media/documents/RESOLUTION_REGARDING_THE_REPUBLICAN_PARTY_PLATFORM.pdf?_ga=2.109560193.504857691.1598219603-2087748323.1598219603.

MADISON CAWTHORN

Bennett, Lynda. "Biography." Published 2020. https://lyndaforcongress.com/biography/.

Bennett, Lynda. "Endorsements." Published 2020. https://lyndaforcongress.com/endorsements/.

Cawthorn, Madison. "About Madison Cawthorn." Accessed October 23, 2020. https://madisoncawthorn.com/about-madison.

Cawthorn, Madison. "Key Policies." Accessed January 18, 2021. https://madisoncawthorn.com/key-policies.

Coaston, Jane. "House Freedom Caucus Founder and Trump Ally Mark Meadows is Retiring From Congress." *Vox*, December 19, 2019. https://www.vox.com/2019/12/19/21029735/mark-meadows-retires.

Crisp, Elizabeth. "North Carolina's Madison Cawthorn, 24, Wants to Shake Up the GOP: 'It's a Culture War.'" *Newsweek*, July 7, 2020. https://www.newsweek.com/north-carolinas-madison-cawthorn-24-wants-shake-gop-its-culture-war-1513179.

Flynn, Meagan. "A 24-year-old Novice Beat a Trump-endorsed Candidate in Primary Race for Mark Meadows's Seat in Congress." *The Washington Post*, published June 24, 2020. https://www.washingtonpost.com/nation/2020/06/24/madison-cawthorn-meadows-election/.

Hess, Abigail. "29-year-old Alexandria Ocasio-Cortez Makes History as the Youngest Woman Ever Elected to Congress." *CNBC*, November 7, 2018. https://www.cnbc.com/2018/11/06/alexandria-ocasio-cortez-is-now-the-youngest-woman-elected-to-congress.html.

Mack, David. "Most of Gen Z Leans Left, but Their First Member of Congress Will Probably Be Way to the Right." *BuzzFeed News*, June 27, 2020. https://www.buzzfeednews.com/article/davidmack/madison-cawthorn-gen-z-congress-youngest-north-carolina.

McLaughlin, Kelly. "Republican Rep. Madison Cawthorn Told a Turning Point USA Crowd Last Month to 'Lightly Threaten' Lawmakers If They Didn't Support Claims of Voter Fraud." *Business Insider*, January 12, 2021. https://www.businessinsider.com/gop-rep-cawthorn-told-supporters-lightly-threaten-lawmakers-voter-fraud-2021-1.

Murphy, Brian. "24-year-old Defeats Candidate Backed by Trump, Meadows in GOP Congressional Primary." *The Charlotte Observer*, June 23, 2020. https://www.charlotteobserver.com/news/politics-government/article243752012.html/.

Nguyen, Tina. "Trump Keeps Fighting a Confederate Flag Battle Many Supporters Have Conceded." *Politico*, July 18, 2020. https://www.politico.com/news/2020/07/18/trump-confederate-flag-battle-368607.

Nuzzi, Olivia. "What Madison Cawthorn Saw at the Insurrection." *Intelligencer*, January 16, 2021. https://nymag.com/intelligencer/2021/01/madison-cawthorn-capitol-insurrection-washington.html.

OpenSecrets. "North Carolina District 11 Race." Published October 22, 2020. https://www.opensecrets.org/races/summary?-cycle=2020&id=NC11.

Parker, Kim, and Ruth Igielnik. "On the Cusp of Adulthood and Facing an Uncertain Future: What We Know about Gen Z So Far." *Pew Research Center*, May 14, 2020. https://www.pewsocialtrends.org/essay/on-the-cusp-of-adulthood-and-facing-an-uncertain-future-what-we-know-about-gen-z-so-far/.

U.S. Constitution, art. I, sec. 2.

WOMEN AND POLITICS

Baird, Julia. "Sarah Palin and Women Voters." *Newsweek*, September 12, 2008. https://www.newsweek.com/sarah-palin-and-women-voters-88503.

Blazina, Carrie Elizabeth, and Drew DeSilver. "A Record Number of Women are Serving in the 117th Congress." *Pew Research Center*, January 15, 2021. https://www.pewresearch.org/fact-tank/2021/01/15/a-record-number-of-women-are-serving-in-the-117th-congress/.

Carlin, Diana B. and Kelly L. Winfrey. "Have You Come a Long Way, Baby? Hillary Clinton, Sarah Palin, and Sexism in 2008 Campaign Coverage." *Communication Studies* 60, no. 4 (September-October 2009). https://doi.org/10.1080/10510970903109904.

Cummings, Laura and Jenepher Lennox Terrion. "A "Nasty Woman": Assessing the Gendered Mediation of Hillary Clinton's Nonverbal Immediacy Cues during the 2016 U.S. Presidential Campaign." *Feminist Media Studies* 20, no. 8 (January 2020). https://doi.org/10.1080/14680777.2019.1706604.

Davis, Susan. "Record Number of Women Run for Congress in 2020." *NPR*, June 16, 2020. https://www.npr. org/2020/06/16/878852938/record-number-of-women-run-for-congress-in-2020.

Frerking, Beth, and John F. Harris. "Clinton Aides: Palin Treatment Sexist." *Politico*, September 3, 2008. https://www.politico.com/ story/2008/09/clinton-aides-palin-treatment-sexist-013129.

Jamieson, Kathleen Hall. *Beyond the Double Bind: Women and Leadership*. Oxford, England: Oxford University Press, 1995.

Lee, MJ. "Trump's Accusers: 'The Forgotten' Women of the #MeToo Movement." *CNN*, July 19, 2019. https://www.cnn. com/2019/07/19/politics/donald-trump-accusers-me-too-movement/index.html.

Lerer, Lisa, and Sydney Ember. "Kamala Harris Makes History as First Woman and Woman of Color as Vice President." *The New York Times*, January 11, 2021. https://www.nytimes. com/2020/11/07/us/politics/kamala-harris.html.

Lillis, Mike. "Ocasio-Cortez Accosted by GOP Lawmaker Over Remarks: 'That Kind of Confrontation Hasn't Ever Happened to Me." *The Hill*, July 21, 2020. https://thehill.com/homenews/ house/508259-ocaasio-cortez-accosted-by-gop-lawmaker-over-remarks-that-kind-of.

Milligan, Susan. "A Historic Day, a Familiar Refrain." *U.S. News & World Report*, August 14, 2020. https://www.usnews.com/news/elections/articles/2020-08-14/kamala-harris-faces-familiar-sexist-remarks-after-joining-the-ticket.

Mondale, Walter. "Geraldine Ferraro." *TIME*, April 11, 2011. http://content.time.com/time/magazine/article/0,9171,2062559,00.html.

Parker, Kim, Nikki Graf, and Ruth Igielnik. "Generation Z Looks a Lot Like Millennials on Key Social and Political Issues." *Pew Research Center*, January 17, 2019. https://www.pewsocialtrends.org/2019/01/17/generation-z-looks-a-lot-like-millennials-on-key-social-and-political-issues/.

Raju, Manu. "Ocasio-Cortez Reveals New Details about Viral Incident with Rep. Ted Yoho." *CNN*, July 24, 2020. https://www.cnn.com/2020/07/24/politics/aoc-ted-yoho-latest/index.html.

Remnick, David. "Alexandria Ocasio-Cortez Delivers a Lesson in Decency on the House Floor." *The New Yorker*, July 24, 2020. https://www.newyorker.com/news/daily-comment/alexandria-ocasio-cortez-ted-yoho-lesson-in-decency-on-the-house-floor.

Rubin, Jennifer. "Women Launch a Shot across the Media's Bow." *The Washington Post*, August 7, 2020. https://www.washingtonpost.com/opinions/2020/08/07/women-launch-shot-across-medias-bow.

R.W. "Geraldine Ferraro." *The Economist*, March 27, 2011. https://www.economist.com/democracy-in-america/2011/03/27/geraldine-ferraro.

Zheng, Wei, Ronit Kark, and Alyson Meister. "How Women Manage the Gendered Norms of Leadership." *Harvard Business Review*, November 28, 2018. https://hbr.org/2018/11/how-women-manage-the-gendered-norms-of-leadership.

LATINX VOTERS

Barroso, Amanda. "Gen Z Eligible Voters Reflect the Growing Racial and Ethnic Diversity of U.S. Electorate." *Pew Research Center*, September 23, 2020. https://www.pewresearch.org/fact-tank/2020/09/23/gen-z-eligible-voters-reflect-the-growing-racial-and-ethnic-diversity-of-u-s-electorate/.

Cadava, Geraldo L.. "How Trump Grew His Support among Latinos." *The Atlantic*, November 9, 2020. https://www.theatlantic.com/ideas/archive/2020/11/how-trump-grew-his-support-among-latinos/617033/.

Jacobson, Louis. "Beto O'Rourke on Target about Scale of Democratic Surge in Texas in 2018." *PolitiFact*, June 24, 2019. https://www.politifact.com/factchecks/2019/jun/24/beto-orourke/beto-orourke-target-about-scale-democratic-surge-t/.

Karas, Tania. "Every 30 Seconds, a Young Latino in the U.S. Turns 18. Their Votes Count More Than Ever." *High Plains Public Radio*, March 10, 2020. https://www.hppr.org/post/every-30-seconds-young-latino-us-turns-18-their-votes-count-more-ever.

Krogstad, Jens Manuel, Ana Gonzalez-Barrera, and Christina Tamer. "Latino Democratic Voters Place High Importance on 2020 Presidential Election." *Pew Research Center*, January 17,

2020. https://www.pewresearch.org/fact-tank/2020/01/17/latino-democratic-voters-place-high-importance-on-2020-presidential-election/.

Krogstad, Jens Manuel, Antonia Flores, and Mark Hugo Lopez. "Key Takeaways about Latino Voters in the 2018 Midterm Elections." *Pew Research Center,* November 9, 2018. https://www.pewresearch.org/fact-tank/2018/11/09/how-latinos-voted-in-2018-midterms/.

Narea, Nicole, and Dylan Scott. "The Price—and Big Potential Payoff—of Turning Texas Blue." *Vox,* September 21, 2020. https://www.vox.com/policy-and-politics/21417460/texas-blue-democrat-biden-beto-2020-election.

Patten, Eileen. "The Nation's Latino Population is Defined by Its Youth." *Pew Research Center,* April 20, 2016. https://www.pewresearch.org/hispanic/2016/04/20/the-nations-latino-population-is-defined-by-its-youth/.

Stokes-Brown, Atiya. "The Latino Vote in the 2016 Election-Myths and Realities of the 'Trump Effect.'" In *Conventional Wisdom, Parties, and Broken Barriers in the 2016 Election,* edited by Jennifer C. Lucas, Christopher J. Galdieri, and Tauna Starbuck Siscom, 64. Lanham, Maryland: Lexington Books, 2018.

Tufts University Center for Information and Research on Civic Learning and Engagement. "County by County, Youth of Color Key to Democrats in 2018." Published November 12, 2018. https://circle.tufts.edu/latest-research/election-week-2020#youth-voting:-state-by-state.

United States Census Bureau. "QuickFacts: Texas." Accessed
November 20, 2020. https://www.census.gov/quickfacts/fact/
table/TX/POP010210.

The World Staff. "Meet the Young Latino voters of 'Every 30 Seconds.'" *The World*, June 11, 2020. https://www.pri.
org/stories/2020-06-10/meet-young-latino-voters-every-30-seconds.

VOTING HABITS

Cilluffo, Anthony, and Richard Fry. "Gen Z, Millennials and
Gen X outvoted older generations in 2018 midterms." *Pew
Research Center*, May 29, 2019. https://www.pewresearch.org/
fact-tank/2019/05/29/gen-z-millennials-and-gen-x-outvoted-
older-generations-in-2018-midterms/.

De Tocqueville, Alexis. *Democracy in America*. Chicago, IL: University of Chicago Press, 2000.

Della Volpe, John. "The Role of Young Voters in 2020." Interview
by Kerri Miller, *MPR News with Kerri Miller,* MPR News, April
27, 2020, audio, 50:02.

Edwards, Sarah. "Talking Elections." October 19, 2018, in *Talk
Policy To Me,* podcast, 27:54. https://gspp.berkeley.edu/news/
podcast/episode-2-4-talking-about-young-voters.

Graf, Nikki, Ruth Igielnik, and Kim Parker. "Generation Z Looks
a Lot Like Millennials on Key Social and Political Issues." *Pew
Research Center,* January 17, 2019. https://www.pewsocialtrends.
org/2019/01/17/generation-z-looks-a-lot-like-millennials-on-
key-social-and-political-issues/

Hansen, Claire. "Young Voters Turned Out in Historic Numbers, Early Estimates Show." *U.S. News*, November 7, 2018. https://www.usnews.com/news/politics/articles/2018-11-07/young-voters-turned-out-in-historic-numbers-early-estimates-show.

Kendi, Ibram X. "Stop Blaming Young Voters for Not Turning Out for Sanders." *The Atlantic*, March 17, 2020. (article) https://www.theatlantic.com/ideas/archive/2020/03/stop-blaming-young-voters-not-turning-out-sanders/608137/.

Kight, Stef W. "Deep Dive: 2020's New Voters Will Usher in an Age of Demographic Transformation." *Axios*, December 14, 2019. https://www.axios.com/2020s-new-voters-demographic-transformation-9da0acc7-0a30-447d-a4a2-4ef66640eee9.html.

Mackinac Center for Public Policy. "The Overton Window." Accessed May 28, 2020. https://www.mackinac.org/Overton-Window.

Misra, Jordan. "Voter Turnout Rates among All Voting Age and Major Racial and Ethnic Groups Were Higher Than in 2014." *United States Census Bureau*, last modified April 23, 2019. https://www.census.gov/library/stories/2019/04/behind-2018-united-states-midterm-election-turnout.html.

Post, Matt. "What Do Young Voters Want?" Interview by James Morrison and Amanda Williams. *Across America*, 1A, February 6, 2019, audio, 29:50. https://www.mprnews.org/episode/2020/04/27/the-role-of-young-voters-in-2020.

Romero, Mindy. "Why Is Youth Voter Turnout So Low?" Filmed May 2016 in Davis, California. YouTube video, 15:23. https://www.youtube.com/watch?v=T2jwSUhu7ok.

Taylor, Kate. "Gen Z is More Conservative Than Many Realize—but the Instagram-Fluent Generation Will Revolutionize the Right." *Business Insider*, 2019. https://www.businessinsider.com/gen-z-changes-political-divides-2019-7.

Tuft University CIRCLE. "Election Week 2020: Young People Increase Turnout, Lead Biden to Victory." Published November 25, 2020. https://circle.tufts.edu/latest-research/election-week-2020#young-voters-and-youth-of-color-powered-biden-victory.

"Young and New Voters Surge in Early Voting." *The Hill*, October 31, 2018. https://thehill.com/homenews/campaign/414098-young-and-new-voters-surge-in-early-voting.

FEEL THE BERN

Aisch, Gregor, Josh Katz, Josh Keller, and Alicia Parlapiano. "Clinton's Growing Delegate Lead Is Nearly Unbeatable." *The New York Times*, March 16, 2016. https://www.nytimes.com/interactive/2016/03/16/upshot/clinton-sanders-democratic-delegate-lead.html.

Berman, Russell. "Was the Iowa Caucus Decided by Coin Flips." *The Atlantic*, February 2, 2016. https://www.theatlantic.com/politics/archive/2016/02/hillary-clinton-bernie-sanders-coin-flips-iowa-caucus/459429/.

Delli Carpini, Michael X.. "Gen.com: Youth, Civic Engagement, and the New Information Environment." *Political Communication* 17, no. 4, (2000), 341-349. https://doi.org/10.1080/10584600050178942.

Detrow, Scott. "8 Key Moments That Helped Define Bernie Sanders' Presidential Runs." *NPR*, April 9, 2020. https://www.npr.org/2020/04/09/830728501/8-key-moments-that-helped-define-bernie-sanders-presidential-runs.

Keith, Tamara. "Bernie Sanders 'Stunned' by Large Crowds Showing up for Him." *NPR*, June 15, 2015. https://www.npr.org/sections/itsallpolitics/2015/06/15/414689799/bernie-sanders-stunned-by-large-crowds-showing-up-for-him.

THE AOC EFFECT

Alexandria Ocasio-Cortez. Interview by Stephen Colbert, *The Late Show with Stephen Colbert*. June 28, 2018. https://www.youtube.com/watch?v=Y_1G4_oPt_o.

Arkin, James, and Scott Bland. "Top Democrat Crowley Loses in Shocker." *Politico*, June 26, 2018. https://www.politico.com/story/2018/06/26/new-york-primary-election-results-2018-updates-677637.

Ben Shapiro. Interview by Martha MacCallum, *The Story with Martha MacCallum*. June 27, 2018. (episode) https://insider.foxnews.com/2018/06/27/ben-shapiro-alexandria-ocasio-cortez-beating-joe-crowley-new-york-democrat-primary.

Crowley for Congress. "Endorsements." Accessed July 20, 2020. https://crowleyforcongress.com/?page_id=467.

Foran, Clare. "Alexandria Ocasio-Cortez Wins Democratic Primary Against Michelle Caruso-Cabrera, CNN Projects." CNN, June 24, 2020. https://www.cnn.com/2020/06/23/politics/aoc-ny-primary-14th-district/index.html.

Remnick, David. "Alexandria Ocasio-Cortez's Historic Win and the Future of the Democratic Party." *The New Yorker*, July 16, 2018. https://www.newyorker.com/magazine/2018/07/23/alexandria-ocasio-cortezs-historic-win-and-the-future-of-the-democratic-party.

Tucker Carlson, "AOC Has the Cure for Human Extinction." April 1, 2019, on *Tucker Carlson Tonight*, video, *5:30*. https://www.foxnews.com/opinion/tucker-carlson-heres-why-awful-ocasio-cortez-has-a-following-and-its-not-because-shes-impressive.

ON THE GROUND

Brooks, David. "The Age of Coddling Is Over." *The New York Times,* April 16, 2020. https://www.nytimes.com/2020/04/16/opinion/coronavirus-medical-training.html.

Brownstein, Ronald. "The Rage Unifying Boomers and Gen Z." *The Atlantic*, June 18, 2020. https://www.theatlantic.com/politics/archive/2020/06/todays-protest-movements-are-as-big-as-the-1960s/613207/.

Busby, Joshua W. "Who Cares about the Weather?: Climate Change and U.S. National Security." *Security Studies* 17, no. 3 (September 2008): 468-504. https://doi.org/10.1080/09636410802319529.

Davis, Dominic-Madori. "The Action Generation: How Gen Z Really Feels about Race, Equality, and Its Role in the Historic George Floyd Protests, Based on a Survey of 39,000 Young Americans." *Business Insider,* June 10, 2020. https://www.businessinsider.com/how-gen-z-feels-about-george-floyd-protests-2020-6..

Kiersz, Andy. "Americans over Age 65 Run the Country. Here Are 7 Charts That Show How They Hold More Power Than Everyone Else." *Business Insider,* November 4, 2020. https://www.businessinsider.com/charts-show-how-older-americans-hold-power-2020-11.

Wallace-Wells, David. *The Uninhabitable Earth: Life After Warming.* New York: Crown, 2020.

MALALA

Botelho, Greg, and Aliza Kassim. "Pakistan: 2 Convicted, 8 Acquitted in Connection to Malala Yousafzai Attack." *CNN World,* June 5, 2015. https://www.cnn.com/2015/06/05/world/asia/malala-attackers-eight-sentences-overturned/index.html.

Yousafazi, Malala. "Malala Yousafzai: Our Books and Our Pens are the Most Powerful Weapons." *The Guardian,* July 12, 2013. https://www.theguardian.com/commentisfree/2013/jul/12/malala-yousafzai-united-nations-education-speech-text.

"Malala Yousafazai: Pakistan Activist, 14, shot in Swat," *BBC*, published October 9, 2012. https://www.bbc.com/news/world-asia-23241937.

The Nobel Prize. "Malala Yousafzai." Accessed October 23, 2020. https://www.nobelprize.org/prizes/peace/2014/yousafzai/facts/.

UNESCO. "Malala Day." Accessed October 23, 2020. https://en.unesco.org/events/malala-day.

UNICEF. "Malala Addresses Youth Delegates in UN." Published July 12, 2013. https://www.unicef.ie/stories/one-child-one-teacher-one-book-and-one-pen-can-change-the-world.

United States Department of State. "Country Reports on Terrorism 2016 - Foreign Terrorist Organizations: Tehrik-e Taliban Pakistan (TTP)." Published July 19, 2017. https://www.refworld.org/docid/5981e3bd26.html.

Walsh, Declan. "Taliban Gun down Girl Who Spoke up for Rights." *New York Times*, October 9, 2012. https://www.nytimes.com/2012/10/10/world/asia/teen-school-activist-malala-yousafzai-survives-hit-by-pakistani-taliban.html.

THE PARKLAND KIDS

Almsay, Steve. "March for Our Lives: Top Moments That Made up a Movement." *CNN*, March 25, 2018. https://www.cnn.com/2018/03/24/us/march-for-our-lives-wrap/index.html.

Booker, Brakkton. "After Parkland, Young Voters Were Galvanized, Activists Vow to Continue to Organize." *NPR*, November 8, 2018. https://www.npr.org/2018/11/08/665547189/youth-vote-and-gun-control-in-florida.

Daugherty, Alex. "Youth Voter Registration Went up 41 Percent in Florida After Parkland." *Miami Herald*, July 19, 2018. https://www.miamiherald.com/news/politics-government/article215169905.html.

Harvard Kennedy School Institute of Politics. "Harvard IOP Youth Poll Finds Stricter Gun Laws, Ban on Assault Weapons Favored by Two-thirds of Likely Midterm Voters under Age 30." Published Spring 2018. https://iop.harvard.edu/about/newsletter-press-release/harvard-iop-youth-poll-finds-stricter-gun-laws-ban-assault-weapons.

Kirby, Jen. "The National School Walkout, Explained." *Vox*, March 14, 2018. https://www.vox.com/policy-and-politics/2018/3/13/17110044/national-school-walkout-day.

Samee Ali, Safia. "Rubio Grilled by Parkland Shooting Survivors, Parents." *NBC News*, February 22, 2018. https://www.nbcnews.com/news/us-news/rubio-grilled-parkland-shooting-students-parent-n850176.

Witt, Emily. "How the Survivors of Parkland Began the Never Again Movement." *The New Yorker,* February 19, 2018. https://www.newyorker.com/news/news-desk/how-the-survivors-of-parkland-began-the-never-again-movement.

CDC. "Estimated Disease Burden of COVID-19." Updated January 19, 2021. https://www.cdc.gov/coronavirus/2019-ncov/cases-updates/burden.html.

CDC. "Trends in Number of COVID-19 Cases and Deaths in the US Reported to CDC, by State/Territory." Accessed January 29, 2021. https://covid.cdc.gov/covid-data-tracker/#trends_daily-trendsdeaths.

Clark, Dartunorro. "Trump Suggests 'Injection' of Disinfectant to Beat Coronavirus and 'Clean' the Lungs." NBC News, April 23, 2020. https://www.nbcnews.com/politics/donald-trump/trump-suggests-injection-disinfectant-beat-coronavirus-clean-lungs-n1191216.

The Editors of Encyclopaedia Britannica."Pearl Harbor Attack." Encyclopaedia Brittanica, updated November 30, 2020. https://www.britannica.com/event/Pearl-Harbor-attack.

Gangel, Jamie, Jeremy Herb, and Elizabeth Stuart. "'Play It Down': Trump Admits to Concealing the True Threat of Coronavirus in New Woodward Book." CNN, September 9, 2020. https://www.cnn.com/2020/09/09/politics/bob-woodward-rage-book-trump-coronavirus/index.html.

Glanz, James, and Campbell Robertson. "Lockdown Delays Cost at Least 36,000 Lives, Data Shows." The New York Times, May 20, 2020. https://www.nytimes.com/2020/05/20/us/coronavirus-distancing-deaths.html.

Johnson, Lauren M. "New York City Spent Two Minutes Clapping for Coronavirus First Responders." *CNN,* March 27, 2020. https://www.cnn.com/2020/03/27/us/new-york-claps-for-first-responders-trnd/index.html.

Moreland, Amanda, Christine Herlihy, Michael A. Tynan, Gregory Sunshine, Russell F. McCord, Charity Hilton, Jason Poovey, Angela K. Werner, Christopher D. Jones, Erika B. Fulmer, Adi V. Gundlapalli, Heather Strosnider, Aaron Potvien, Macarena C. García, Sally Honeycutt, and Grant Baldwin. "Timing of State and Territorial COVID-19 Stay-at-Home Orders and Changes in Population Movement—United States, March 1 - May 31, 2020." *Morbidity and Mortality Weekly Report* 69, no. 35 (September 2020), 1198-1203. http://dx.doi.org/10.15585/mmwr.mm6935a2.

WHERE DO WE GO FROM HERE?

Abovian, Ellina. "From Plastic Zip-tie Handcuffs to Pipe Bombs, Sinister Nature of Assault on the Capitol Is Coming into Focus." *KTLA,* January 11, 2021. https://ktla.com/news/nation-world/assault-on-u-s-capitol-much-more-sinister-than-1st-appeared/.

Anishanslin, Zara. "What We Get Wrong about Ben Franklin's 'a Republic, If You Can Keep It.'" *The Washington Post,*October 29, 2019. https://www.washingtonpost.com/outlook/2019/10/29/what-we-get-wrong-about-ben-franklins-republic-if-you-can-keep-it/.

Diaz, Johnny. "Biden Is the Oldest President to Take the Oath." *The New York Times,* January 18, 2021. https://www.nytimes.

com/2021/01/18/us/politics/joe-biden-age-oldest-presidents. html.

Fandos, Nicholas. "Trump Impeached for Inciting Insurrection." *The New York Times*, January 13, 2021. https://www. nytimes.com/2021/01/13/us/politics/trump-impeached.html.

Jones, Zoe Christen. "Amanda Gorman Reads 'The Hill We Climb' at Biden's Inauguration." *CBS News*, January 21, 2021. https:// www.cbsnews.com/news/amanda-gorman-inauguration-poem-the-hill-we-climb-reading/.

Kane, Paul. "Senate's Octogenarians Face the Age Question and Whether It's Time to Exit." *The Washington Post*, December 12, 2020. https://www.washingtonpost.com/powerpost/senate-age-grassley-mecconnell-feinstein/2020/12/11/1f-33b60a-3bd3-11eb-9276-ae0ca72729be_story.html.

Leonhardt, David. "Inside the Capitol Attack." *The New York Time*, January 19, 2021. https://www.nytimes.com/2021/01/19/briefing/trump-biden-brazil-1776-report.html.

Rogers, Luke. "Counties Can Have the Same Median Age but Very Different Population Distributions." *United States Census Bureau*, June 20, 2019. https://www.census.gov/library/stories/2019/06/median-age-does-not-tell-the-whole-story.html.

Sherman, Gabriel. "'They're Being Told to Stay Away from Trump': After a Day of Violence and 25th Amendment Chatter, Trump's Allies Are Jumping Ship." *Vanity Fair*, January 7, 2021. https://www.vanityfair.com/news/2021/01/after-a-day-of-violence-and-25th-amendment-chatter-trumps-allies-jump-ing-ship?itm_content=footer-recirc.

Swan, Jonathan, and Zachary Basu. "Episode 8: The Siege." *Axios*, January 21, 2021. https://www.axios.com/off-the-rails-trump-capitol-siege-601f6ff0-7465-4da7-9669-4629fb14f477.html.

The Washington Post Fact Checker. "In Four Years, President Trump Made 30,573 False or Misleading Claims." *The Washington Post*, updated January 20, 2021. https://www.washingtonpost.com/graphics/politics/trump-claims-database/?tid=pm_graphics_pop_b.

Wilson, Reid. "Biden Faces 100 Days of Crisis." *The Hill*, January 20, 2021. https://thehill.com/homenews/administration/535003-biden-faces-100-days-of-crisis.

Zak, Dan. "Joe Biden, 78, Will Lead an American Gerontocracy." *The Washington Post*, January 12, 2021. https://www.washingtonpost.com/lifestyle/style/joe-biden-age-oldest-president/2021/01/12/91353560-49fe-11eb-839a-cf4ba7b7c48c_story.html.

Made in the USA
Monee, IL
09 May 2021